The Most Interesting Man You Have Never Met

Tom West

McGilligan Publishing
3707 Cypress Creek Pkwy Ste 310 #505
Houston, TX 77068

THE MOST INTERESTING MAN YOU HAVE NEVER MET

TOM WEST

MCGILLIGAN PUBLISHING

3707 CYPRESS CREEK PKWY STE 310 #505

HOUSTON, TX 77068

WWW.MCGILLIGANPUBLISHING.COM

COPYRIGHT © 2025

ISBN

HARDCOVER: 978-1-965560-90-7

PAPERBACK: 978-1-965560-91-4

PRINTED IN THE UNITED STATES OF AMERICA

Second Edition

Contents

ᴄ/᾿Introduction☙

I t is the summer of 2007, and the vacation we planned for five months is finally here. Been waiting a long time—so it seemed for this day.

On Saturday, July 7th, with the camp trailer loaded and the motorcycle tucked safely in the pickup bed, we left for June Lake, California. June Lake is one of several lakes in the Sierra Nevada Mountains located in the east-central part of the State. It has become our go-to place in the hot summer of Las Vegas, Nevada.

The six-hour drive was a relief, to say the least, after all the planning and marking off the calendar for three months. This was to be a vacation of relaxing, fishing, riding the motorcycle, and just doing nothing but kicking back and forgetting the last year.

The first few days were great. We fished, rode the motorcycle, read, drank, and ate until Friday, when we headed to Reno for the weekend. My cousin in Oregon said they would travel to Reno to meet with us, and we were excited about seeing them and catching up on everything.

So, on Friday, after buttoning up the trailer and securing the motorcycle, we jumped into the pickup headed for Reno. On the way, my cousin called to let us know they thought they would be in Reno at about six that evening. Already on the road, around noon, we decided to drive to Virginia City, Nevada. We wanted to see what Virginia City, an old western mining town, looked like and it was on the way, sort of, to Reno.

i

When we got to town, we parked the truck in a little parking lot situated at the edge of a cliff right in downtown. Excited to see what this city was all about, we started across the parking lot. As we did, I started having the worst pain I think I have ever experienced in my life, going across my right hip and down my leg. I sat down on a bench, which eased the pain, and after a few minutes, we went across the street, where I had to sit down again because of the pain. To say the least, the visit to Virginia City wasn't going well with the pain I was experiencing. But I kept trying to walk it off.

Leaving Virginia City, we headed to Reno and checked into the hotel/casino. Shortly after that, Cousin Curt and his wife showed up. We had dinner and tried to play some slot machines while visiting. But the pain in my hip and leg continued throughout the evening. It was really hard to walk any distance without hurting more than a broken arm. After a while, we decided to go to our room so I could lie down and maybe stop the pain. We told Curt that we would catch up with them in the morning for breakfast.

Lying down did help. I rested okay during the night, and the next morning decided to go to the hotel lobby to get some coffee at a little shop like a Starbucks. I didn't make it; the pain came back with a vengeance and was so intense that I barely hobbled back to the room.

When I got into the room, Diana, my wife, took one look at me and helped me back to bed.

She said, "You are going to a doctor to see what is going on." She was very worried about what was going on. Being in a city we were not familiar with, she told me she was going to the hotel desk to see where an Urgent Care was located.

She spoke with the Security Officer on duty and explained the problem. All she wanted was to know where to take me, but the Security Officer told her THEY would take us to the Emergency Room. The Security Department sent two people with a wheelchair to our room. They loaded me into it and proceeded to take me to the hospital that was only two blocks away.

Once in the ER and after completing paperwork, the physician's assistant came into the room and asked me if the pain just went down my leg to the knee or did it travel further down my leg. I told him the pain went all the way to my right foot. He then called the doctor, and they ordered x-rays of my back.

The doctor, his assistant, and the radiologist came back into the room with the X-rays. The doctor asked me how long I had known of the very severe form of disc disease in my back. I told him that I guess I'm hearing about it for the first time right now. The doctor then asked me what kind of work I did. I told the doctor that I was a card dealer at Wynn Las Vegas. His statement back to me has changed my life. He told me I should consider retiring. He explained that with this condition, I would not be able to stand for six or seven hours a day, for this condition would only get worse. If I wanted to have some quality of life, I needed to make a major change now.

I was released, and after stopping by the pharmacy to get pain pills, we found Curt and Carolyn and explained what happened at the ER.

The pills helped a bit, but there was no sense in staying at the hotel. If I walked any distance, the pain came back. We decided to leave and head back to June Lake. Diana drove us from Reno to our spot at June Lake.

For the next three days, I sat in a lawn chair and thought about what to do next. We went fishing a couple of times, but the fishing was very slow. The lack of snow that winter had left the lakes a little short on water. Most of the time, I just sat in the lawn chair, feeding peanuts to the little chipmunks and thinking about my future.

Retirement was a word I wasn't too sure what the meaning really was. I had known lots of retired people including my parents, but just what was this retired thing going to be like for me? I had some money, not broke by any means, and I could get social security and maybe disability. I had purchased disability insurance where I worked. My wife had a good job and we would not go hungry and live in the street. But the idea of being retired and not going to work every day was something I had never really put much thought into. The more I sat and looked at the pine trees and threw peanuts to the chippies, the more my mind raced into the future. I wouldn't have to get up and go to work every morning, so what the heck was I going to do with myself each day? I have always been long on ideas, so this might not be such a problem.

Ok, so we went home the next Wednesday, and I did just that, retired. This is where the story ends; oh, I hope it doesn't end here. I hope it is a new and just as exciting chapter in what I have been told many times is one very, very interesting life, but the beginning started some sixty-three years ago.

ᑽᎡᏮᎥᏮᏮᏮ One ᎪᏮᏮᏮᏮ
ᑽᎡᏮᎥᏮᏮᏮ Chapter One ᎪᏮᏮᏮᏮ

I t was the summer of 1944, and World War II was hopefully coming to an end. The Normandy invasion had been just a month ago, in June, and the war was continuing to rage in Asia as well as in Europe.

It was during this same time that I was born on July 9, 1944. My father was in the army and my mother had been a schoolteacher in southwestern Oklahoma. I was born in the same town where my parents had lived—Fredrick, Oklahoma. Fredrick is a small town in the southwest of Oklahoma with very little industry except farming, ranching, and oil.

Arlie, my dad, had been drafted in 1942 and was sent to boot camp at Fort Carson, Colorado. While he was there, Mom traveled from Fredrick, and they got married on October 2, 1942. After learning to be a soldier for eight weeks, he was sent to Los Angeles, California, to be shipped overseas, as it was called back then.

While waiting to be shipped out, it seems there was a riot at a train station involving some black soldiers. My dad wasn't even there or involved in the situation, but the army sent him back to Fort Carson to go through boot camp again. The army works in mysterious ways is the only explanation given at the time. With experience of two boot camps under his belt and the fact that the Colonel was also named West, well, dear old Dad made Sergeant and Drill Instructor for the next boot camp. Having been in the army for a year and a half, he was still in Colorado.

Shortly after I was born, the army sent my dad from Colorado to Durham, North Carolina. My mother decided to take me to Durham so we could see him. I was only a few months old and was traveling by train to the East Coast. In 1944, this was very unusual. Most people in the country did not travel over a couple hundred miles from where they were born.

And World War II put a lot of hardships on most people. Sugar was rationed, along with just about everything else. My dad would say, "Yes, sugar is rationed; use as little as possible and stir like heck; we don't mind the noise." My dad had many sayings that sometimes had to be heard a couple of times to get the meaning. If not, they'd ask some silly question about what they heard him say.

Going back to my early days of traveling…Travel was not easy in those days. Most means of travel were used for our soldiers. Now, my mother was trying to go back to Oklahoma from Durham with me in tow, and the only ticket to be had was on a train that was carrying the Ringling Brothers and Barnum & Bailey Circus. The car that mother's seat was in also had passengers from the Circus. One of the passengers was a woman named Baby Betty, the largest woman in the world. This was to be my first encounter of many with a celebrity. Baby Betty wanted to hold me and so she did. We went across the country with me on the lap, or stomach, of the biggest woman in the world.

My mother's parents had moved from Fredrick to Long Beach, California. Within several months of our Durham travels, we went to see my mother's parents in Long Beach. Now, I'm not even a year old and have already traveled to the East Coast, and now I was headed to the West Coast.

My grandfather had a job as a carpenter working in a shipyard in Long Beach, California. Part of the war effort, I guess, and it must have been one of the only jobs to be had in

1945. I never found out why they moved from Oklahoma to Long Beach, but they did. We stayed there until I got sick with an ear infection that would not go away. The doctor my mother was taking me to told her I needed to get out of the area for me to get well. Back in Oklahoma, I was still getting ear infections, so at eighteen months old, I had my tonsils taken out.

Back in Oklahoma, my brother Ronald Lloyd was born on August 8, 1945. He was born in the same hospital I was born in, in Fredrick. Ronny was just thirteen months younger than I. My dad was now in Germany with the occupation army, and I didn't get to see him until the fall of 1945.

The war was over! My dad finally returned to Oklahoma and got a job as manager of the Fredrick Airport. Lots of guys who made it through the war now had no fear of anything. They wanted to learn to fly. So, there was a lot of activity at this little airport. During the war, it was a training base for the B-25 and B-26 bombers. George Goble was one of the flight instructors at this little airbase. Now, in the late 1940s, it had large hangers and big runways, and my dad was the manager.

I started riding in airplanes at a very early age. I rode in about every small airplane in the area. Military trainers, as these airplanes were called, were easy to get when the war was over. My dad and some of his brothers had them, like the PT-19, BT-13, and the PT-17. I rode in them all. It was fun. Heck, I was a cute little kid who was friendly and would say to the pilots, "Take me with you," and they would.

Things are a little different today. Kids wear helmets to ride bikes, and their parents won't even let the kids play in their own neighborhoods. We were riding in stunt planes with strangers, so to speak. Times change, I guess.

I look back on my life and see so much that has changed. But as far as my folks, the changes they saw have been even more dramatic.

My dad's parents came to Oklahoma on a wagon train from eastern Tennessee in the 1890s and settled somewhere around the Fredrick area.

My mother's family moved from Arkansas in 1917 in a covered wagon. The reason the Conway family left Arkansas in a covered wagon was because the KKK was kidnapping little kids and selling them. When three of the hooded fellows knocked on my granny's door, my mother and her sister were hidden under a bed. Granny convinced them there weren't any children there, and they believed her and left. When my grandfather found out what had happened, he decided to move out of the area. The KKK did more than just mess with the blacks in the South.

Now in the late 1940's a lot of oil wells were being drilled in southwestern Oklahoma. Some of these wells had investors like Gene Autry and Jack Dempsey. In 1949, these two celebrities decided to "take a look" at their oil wells. They flew into the airport at Fredrick and enlisted my dad as their guide. Gene Autry was at that time one of the biggest stars in Hollywood. When he got off the plane, he was mobbed. Kids were thick as fleas, and one of them stepped on Gene's shiny silver-toed cowboy boots. Now, ol' Gene was not Roy Rogers by any stretch of the imagination. Roy loved all the fans and was Mr. Nice Guy to everybody in the crowds he met. Gene Autry was not that friendly. He called the kid a "little shit" and walked off to the airplane hangar. This was not something you said to a little kid in southwestern Oklahoma in 1949. I believe his popularity dwindled in Fredrick after that.

The next day, my dad took Gene and Jack to see their oil wells, and there I was again, the cute little kid. I think Gene

4

felt bad about what had happened upon his arrival and decided to try to make it up to me. That day, he carried me around on his shoulders while looking at his wells.

Gene left the next day and went back to Hollywood, but Jack Dempsey stayed for a few days. Jack and my dad became good friends and stayed in touch with each other until the early 1960's.

Jack was standing next to my dad one day looking at a well when Jack said to my dad, "Look at that," and pointed in one direction. When my dad looked toward the way he was pointing, Jack gave my dad a little judo chop on the neck. Dad dropped like a sack of potatoes to the ground. Jack said to my dad, "Now, Arlie, that shows you should not trust someone you just met." Jack Dempsey was somewhat of a joker, and he told my dad now you will be able to tell people you were knocked out by Jack Dempsey. He also told Dad that he didn't mean to hit him that hard.

In 1960, one of the biggest TV shows was The Price Is Right. A friend of my dad tried for six months to get on the show with no success. My dad bet him he could do it in less than one month. Within two weeks after sending in a black postcard with writing in white ink starting out with "The Carbon Black Capital of the World" (we lived in Borger, Texas at the time, and Borger had the largest carbon black plant in the world), my dad received a letter from The Price Is Right show. They asked him to come to New York and be on the show. My dad proceeded to get on an airplane and go to New York. When he got there, I think he chickened out and would not be on the show but sat in the audience. While there, he also went to see Jack Dempsey at his restaurant called Dempsey's Grotto.

I grew up around airplanes and knew them very well as a kid. When my dad was getting on the plane to go to New York City, I noticed that one of the propellers on the Constellation was wobbling. As the passengers were boarding, I told my mother I thought something might be wrong with the engine on the plane. Kids weren't supposed to know about such things, but when the plane landed in Chicago on three engines, I became a little smarter, and people listened to me more often.

Back at the airport where I gained all my experience— there was a fellow named Jim Walker who had an Ariel spraying service at the airport. During WWII, Jim was a fighter pilot who shot down six or seven enemy airplanes, which made him an Ace Fighter Pilot. This was in 1949, and war heroes were still a big deal. Jim had Stearman PT-17s for spray planes, and one day, he didn't have any fields to spray. Jim said to me, "Do you want to go for a ride with me?" I don't think I ever turned down a free ride on an airplane. Jim strapped me in, but at five years old, the shoulder straps didn't quite fit tight on my shoulders.

We taxied down the runway and turned around. Jim looked up at me in the front seat and said, "Hang on, we are going for a real ride." I wished I knew what he was going to do. I took hold of the shoulder straps, thank God, and held on tight as Jim pushed the throttle forward on the PT-17.

Stearman PT-17's came from the factory with a 250-horsepower Jacobs engine. This one had a Pratt and Whitney 450-horsepower engine. Just as the wheels left the ground, Jim rolled the plane upside down and flew the entire length of the runway like that, with me hanging upside down and sliding into the shoulder straps. By the way, the Stearman PT-17 is topless. There was nothing between the shoulder straps and the ground but air and not a heck of a lot of that. I don't really remember what I said at the time, but given the times and the fact that I was only five years old, I don't think it would be what I would say today—"Oh crap."

Riding in airplanes was not only fun and exciting but also a way to get a view of the world from a different perspective than most of the kids of my day. While flying with my dad, one day, we saw a group of men working in a farmer's field.

As I remember, around 1950, in southwestern Oklahoma, most of the black people worked for farmers picking cotton. Well, here were ten or fifteen black people picking cotton. The self-propelled cotton stripper had not been invented yet, and these men were pulling 100-pound cotton sacks with a wide strap that went around their shoulders and dragged on the ground behind them. This left the arms free to pick the cotton bolls. With the sacks more than half-full the men would lean forward to drag the sacks. Given the fact this was usually "bow and air cotton," the men were bent over. "Bow and air cotton" got its name from being so short that to pick it, one had to bow his back and air his ass.

We came from behind the field hands, and my dad dropped the plane down to where the wheels were only about ten feet from the ground. We were aimed at these men with the cotton sacks on their backs doing about 120 miles per hour with a spinning propeller in the front of the airplane.

As we pulled up, I looked back to see most of these men climbing into their cotton sacks or trying to get under them. In 2007, this would not be socially acceptable, nor would calling a black man the N-word. But it was 1950, and nobody really cared except the black cotton pickers who were diving into their cotton sacks.

I could name just about any kind of airplane, car, or tractor available at the time. My grandfather Conway found great fun in asking me to name that car or tractor when we were riding in a car together. I never missed, not in 1950 in southwestern Oklahoma.

Speaking of never missing, I'm not sure when my dad taught me to shoot, but he did at an early age. And I was naturally very good at it. For bragging rights, my dad would have me shoot the head of a kitchen match off at thirty or forty feet away.

Dad had, as he put it, liberated lots of loot in Germany during the war. I'm not sure how he got home with all that loot, but he brought home guns, sabers, scissors, flags, and some items of clothing worn by a German fighter pilot. He brought home two 22 caliber rifles; one was a Mouser single shot, and the other was a Walther single shot, made to look like a K-98 German army rifle. This was the best single-shot rifle I ever saw. I still can't believe that I traded it off in 1969, but I did, and that was that.

Chapter Two

And on to my other adventures and escapades....

My mother's brother Clyde and his wife Doris lived a couple of blocks from us in Fredrick. One day, when we were over at their house, I decided to climb the tree in their front yard. I was on a limb somewhere in the tree and decided to jump to the ground. I landed on a jar that was left by some idiot under that same tree. A piece of the now broken jar went into my foot nearly all the way through. Well, maw took me to the Doctor, and he got the glass out but said it would leave a nasty scar. I don't think I was ever worried about a nasty scar on the bottom of my foot. What I did worry about was that the glass cut something in my foot, which kept me from going without shoes very much after that. I think it cut a tendon or something because going barefoot still hurts some to this day.

I was very adventurous at a very young age. We had a trellis next to the front porch. One day, I tried to climb it to get on top of the house. I did, but I couldn't figure out a way to get down once I got up there. A fireman was nice enough to get me down and then give me my first ride in a fire truck.

In the early summer of 1950, I watched a lineman climb a power pole behind our house in Fredrick. That looked cool. That fellow had spikes on his boots and a big belt around him and the power pole. He could climb all the way to the top of the pole, turn loose with both hands at the same time, and work on the power lines.

Well, heck, if he could do that, so could I. So, I decided to give it a try. I went back into the house, got one of my dad's

9

belts, went back outside, and started climbing the clothesline pole in our backyard. Made it all the way to the top, too. I had the belt around my waist and the clothesline pole. I let go of the pole with both hands, just like the lineman did. The next thing I remember was my mother picking me up and carrying me to the doctor.

I broke both bones in my right wrist and wound up in a cast from my fingertips to my armpit for eight weeks. The first cast of many I would get in the future.

I started school, not kindergarten, but in the first grade in the fall of 1950 at Victory #11. This school was southeast of Fredrick, about eight miles. My mother started teaching again that year. She quit teaching when she married my dad and didn't work again until I started school. The principal's wife babysat my little brother that year.

My mother was very unusual in many ways, one of which was her teaching career. My mother grew up in rural southwestern Oklahoma during the Depression of the 1930s. She and her family moved from Arkansas in 1917 in a covered wagon pulled by horses. Mother finished high school at age fifteen and college at age nineteen and taught school two months before she turned twenty. She and her older sister Doris taught in a two-room school that went to the eighth grade. She told me she had two boys in the 8th grade who were older than her.

When Mother and her sister got the job, one was to be the principal and the other the janitor. These jobs were decided from the flip of a coin. Mother lost the coin toss and was a teacher and janitor. Her sister liked being principal so much that later in her teaching career, she was head of the teachers' school at Louisiana State University and was in the Who's Who of the teaching world. She also had a PhD. My mother stayed as a teacher for over thirty-five years, then retired only to become principal of a high school a few years later. Mother also had her master's in elementary education. The school where she became principal was a Baptist school in Farmington, New Mexico.

At Christmas time that year, there was a party at the principal's house, which was located across the road from the school. Ronny and I went dressed as cowboys, stuff we had gotten for Christmas. When we arrived, we were told to go up to the house and knock on the door. We did as instructed, and when the door opened, we were asked who we were. I, without hesitation, said, "I'm Roy Rogers." Ronny just stood there in silence and was asked again by our host, "Well, who are you, little boy?" Ronny stuttered a little bit and then burst out, "I'm an Indian." Somehow, I don't believe Ronny wanted to be Gene Autry.

The second-grade teacher at Victory #11 school was my mother and I only lasted two weeks in her class. Mother transferred me to the grade school in Fredrick. I think this was a very good idea. I didn't really want my mother for a schoolteacher, even though she was a very good teacher.

I learned a lot in the second grade. Marbles or shooting marbles was the game every boy played in 1951 in southwestern Oklahoma. I became very good at shooting marbles, too good to play with the second graders. I spent most lunchtimes playing with the sixth and seventh graders, shooting marbles, that is. I was good enough to play them but not good enough to beat them most of the time. Marbles was a gambling game where when you lost, you lost your marbles. Maybe that is what is wrong with me today - I lost most of my marbles in the second grade.

You could get a sack of marbles for five cents in 1951 at a store by the name of Tomlinson's. This store later became the first store of the TG&Y variety store chain. TG&Y stood for Tomlinson, Greg, and Young. TG&Y is no longer in business; I think they were bought out in the early 80's.

At the end of the school year in May 1952, our family moved to Borger, Texas. My dad got a job with Phillips Oil Company at the Butadiene Plant there. We moved into a house at 1406 Herbst Street. In the fall of 1952, I started school at Coronado Elementary School.

Some of the friends I made there, which I still have today, are Edie Welch, Jack Alexander, Pat Armstrong, Mike Kelly, and a lot that I have forgotten.

In the fourth grade, we went to East Ward. My mother taught there in the fifth grade. There were two fifth-grade teachers, of which I got the other one, of course.

Now, the fourth grade was where my memory really kicked in, probably because of some of the things we did in those years.

North of Borger there are canyons that go all the way to the Canadian River about ten miles from where we lived. Canyons are what all of us kids called them because of their very rough terrain. There were cliffs and gullies with huge rocks, drop-offs of 100 feet or more, and cliff dishes, as we called them. Cliff dishes were places where water has, over many years, washed out an area that left an overhang, sometimes big enough to stand in. These cliff dishes were where we ate our sandwiches most of the time.

We would leave the house and meet up with the other kids on Saturdays and go hiking in the canyons all day.

There were rattlesnakes, lizards, spiders, and all sorts of critters in those canyons, and one summer, we collected over 100 rattlesnake rattles. Most of them we shot with BB guns.

In 1954, my dad bought a new car. It was a 1954 Mercury Monterey Coupe. The car was a special edition car that had a nameplate on the floorboards that said, "This car was built by The Mercury Division of Ford Motor Co. for Mr. A. F. West of Borger, Texas." The car had a stick shift with an overdrive and a special engine built for racing.

My dad sometimes did brag a little about the stuff he did, and one day, this fellow he worked with challenged my dad to a race. Now, old Dad was not one to back down from anything and quickly accepted the challenge. When he told my mother about the race, she threw a fit. She told him he would not drive the car in a race for forty miles. My dad was not a dummy and quickly said he wasn't going to drive himself. He would get one of the guys that he worked with at Phillips to drive. Well, as it happened, one of the guys that my dad worked with had a son who could drive a racecar. In fact, the son's name was Roger Ward, the one and the same that had just won the Indianapolis 500 the year before. He would drive our car in this race. You can already guess who won the race. The Mercury was very, very fast.

On my tenth birthday, Ronny and I got Daisy Pump BB guns. Most kids had Daisy Red Riders that looked like the 30-30 saddle guns of the old West. We got pumps because the man at the store said to my dad that the pump shot much harder. Well, he was right; the pump shot a lot harder than most of the BB guns of the day. We shot birds, lizards, snakes, and just about anything that moved and a lot of things that didn't move.

My tenth birthday was also the year that we got a TV. Amarillo, Texas, had three TV stations that started in 1954. For a long time, we could only watch the test pattern, but finally, one day, the stations became operational, and we started watching actual programs.

One of the local shows that was very popular during 1954 in Amarillo, Texas, was a kid's show called The Aunt Phyllis Show. Aunt Phyllis had a sidekick named Cagey the Clown. The show had a birthday boy or girl each week, and in July 1954, on my tenth birthday, I was on the show as the birthday boy. Television had only been in Amarillo for a few months, and I was on the thing. Aunt Phyllis said to me on the show, "Wow, our birthday boy sure has big dimples." Not wanting to hog all the applause, I said to Aunt Phyllis, "You should see the dimples my little brother has." The cameraman went to Ronny, who had a big grin on his face, and dimples were all anyone could see. Ronny never had a problem getting girls to look at him. All he had to do was smile with those big dimples, and the girls were hooked.

Back to the canyons… We spent most of our weekends and summers there just stomping around. We hiked these canyons to the point where we knew every rock, nook, and cranny. We packed a lunch, water, and our BB guns and played army, cowboys and Indians, and anything else we could think of. We had a lot of imagination, so the time was just plain fun. We didn't need a computer, video games, or the mall to pass the time; we had friends and lots of fun and games because we had imagination and little money to spend. The canyons were, or became like, a second home to us. We built forts, camps, and playhouses in these canyons and stayed there most of the time when we had nothing else to do. We became such good shots that we could cut a kitchen match in two with one shot from a BB gun at twenty yards.

When I was five or six, my dad would make bets with his friends that I could shoot the head of a kitchen match off with a 22 rifle at twenty yards. We shot so much by the time we were in high school that we probably had killed more varmints than anybody else we had ever heard of. But that was only the start.

14

No one ever got hurt in the canyons except for a few minor scrapes and bruises. We knew what we were doing and how to do it—with one exception. About six of us were in the canyons one Saturday afternoon and we saw from a good distance some other boys coming our way. We knew them and didn't really like them well enough to call them friends. They stopped in a sand wash about a hundred yards from where we were hidden in the rocks. We were at the top of a cliff across the canyon from where these other guys were sitting. Jack had his pump pellet rifle with him. I was holding it, and Jack told me to pump the rifle up about three or four pumps, and we would shoot in front of the others to scare them. I pumped the air rifle up eight to ten times and handed the gun to Jack.

We were all good shots, so we didn't need to aim down the sights for a shot like this one was going to be. We aimed along the side of the barrel and at the target, which was the sand in front of this guy. Jack didn't know that I had pumped the gun up to eight or ten pumps when he pulled the trigger.

Downhill, about 150 feet and twice the power he expected, changed the path of the pellet a lot. In fact, just enough to hit the guy sitting on the rock with his legs spread out. You already know where the pellet hit, don't you? If you think it was in the balls, you are right. What a shot, and from almost 100 yards, but with a 150-foot drop it made a lot of difference in the drop of the pellet. Well, what happened next was funny and not funny. The pellet went through his Levis and shorts. It just broke the skin enough to cause a small amount of blood. The other boys with him found this out when they caught the victim. After falling off the rock he bounced around in the sand a little and was doing all kinds of contortions and using language I had never heard before.

Now, all this time, we were hiding behind the rocks at the top of the cliff, and they had no idea we were there. We were peaking from behind the rocks every so often to see what was going on but were keeping out of sight.

We found out later that he was not really hurt except for his pride and a slight aching between his legs for a day or two. They never found out what happened exactly. I guess the pellet fell down his pants leg and was never found. We laughed and laughed until we hurt on the way back to the house. Jack never figured out why he missed his target of the sand in front of the guy. No one asked about how many pumps the gun had in it when he fired. That was just one day in the canyons, and there were many with wild experiences, maybe not just like that but we never failed to have a good time.

ᢙ∕᷾Chapter Three᷾ᢙ᷾

I n the fall of 1956, I got a bellyache that just wouldn't stop hurting. The next day, it was getting worse, and my mother took me to the doctor. Well, as luck would have it, I had appendicitis and had to have it removed. In 1956, this was not a fun thing, and I stayed in the hospital for five days with this affliction. On the last day in the hospital, there was a knock on the door of my room. This fellow stuck his head in and asked me how I was doing. I told him much better, thanks. This man then came into the room to chat a little. I wish I could remember his name, but he was the commanding general of the United States Air Force, a four-star General.

On March 28, 1957, a Saturday, Ronny and I went to the show at the Rex Theater. We went to the afternoon western as I remember. It was a beautiful spring day in the Texas Panhandle, somewhere in the upper seventies, I guess, as we started home on our bicycles. We had short-sleeved shirts and Levis on. As we were leaving the show, the wind was picking up out of the north; I guessed somewhere about thirty miles per hour. Riding our bicycles in that wind was tough, and the temperature was dropping like a rock. At Tenth Street, we had to get off our bikes and walk because the wind was getting stronger and it was getting very cold. We only had three more blocks to go to get to the house. We were going straight north and looking up at the sky. We could see this huge dark blue cloud that went from horizon to horizon. I remember telling Ronny that we better not stop, or we could freeze right where we stood.

We made it home in a few more minutes and were glad to be out of that wind and cold. Mother asked us, as always, where our coats were. I think this was a standard question in the 1950's. Mothers who grew up poor said things like that so we would think about how we were dressed when we went out. Of course, our answer was it was warm when we left to go to the show.

Well, warm was not a good word for the next couple of days in Borger, Texas. I have seen a lot of storms over the past sixty years, but never like the one in March 1957. Within an hour of our getting home, somewhere about four in the afternoon, the wind was howling at sixty to seventy-plus miles per hour, and it was starting to snow. By around eight o'clock that evening it was snowing so hard you could not see across the street. It was a whiteout like I had never seen before or after. It snowed and blew all night and all the next day.

All Sunday, we stayed in the house and watched the white stuff coming down and swirling around in the wind. The weather station said that the wind on Sunday hit 100 miles per hour many times. In 1957 boys didn't stay in the house come rain or shine all day Sunday unless they were sick. Well, we weren't sick except becoming sick of the wind and snow. We would sit on the bed in Mom and Dad's bedroom and look toward the street. We couldn't see any further than the middle of the yard.

Monday morning finally came. The snow had stopped coming down, and the wind had let up. We went out to see what 100 mph winds and the snow had done to our springtime. It had done a lot. The only way out of the house was the back door. The front porch was full of snow, and I mean full. We dug for an hour just to see where the door was. We gave up on that after an hour of digging because to get the snow shoveled enough to open the front door would have taken another two or three hours of work.

We decided to look around a little because this stuff was totally amazing. It was a little bit wet, so it packed wherever the wind deposited it. From our driveway, we could walk up the snow and be on the roof of our house. Then going south, we could walk to the next house roof, and then the next, and the next. It was pretty cool. When we got to the third house south of us, we just walked down a drift to the yard of the fourth house. If there was no hedgerow at the side of a house, the wind left no snow in the yards. If there was a hedgerow, it made drifts thirty or forty feet to the south.

The house to the north of us had a truck parked in the street. The drift started at the cab of the truck and went north to the corner, one house away. There was a streetlight at the corner, and the drift was so deep that I crawled to the top and could stand up and touch the streetlight. It was not the kind of pole they use today. In 1957, it was a wooden pole like a telephone pole.

The snow was so bad nothing moved for three days in Borger, Texas in the spring of 1957. I have never seen a storm like it ever again and probably never will since I now live in the Mojave Desert.

In a week, we were wearing short-sleeved shirts again. Springtime brought windy and stormy weather to the Texas Panhandle. I can't remember too many years that we didn't have tornado warnings at least once in the spring and early summer.

That year, Dad bought a house, and we moved. It was north of where we had lived for four years and just west of the traffic circle at the north end of Borger on Boyd Street. The house wasn't much different from our old house except it was ours and it was newer and was a brick house. Brick houses were a big step up from the houses in the old neighborhood. Most of the houses in Borger were not brick, so this was a major improvement. At least, that was what my Dad said many times.

Ronny and I got the bedroom off the front of the house, and we could fix things the way we wanted... another improvement over living in a rented house. The backyard was larger, and the first year, we planted very good grass. In those days, money was not what it is today and wasn't spent on stuff like grass seed. So, we planted the back yard in sprigs of grass taken from the front yard. This was Bermuda grass, and it spread like wildfire and covered the entire yard in a year. We also built a fence in the backyard and a brick barbeque pit with a fireplace. We had one of the coolest backyards in the neighborhood.

In the fall of 1956, I started school at Sam Houston Junior High. Sometime before school started for the year, the school that the black kids went to burned down. I guess the school district didn't have the money to rebuild the school, so the black kids went to our high school and junior high. This was in 1956 in Texas, the hardcore south. But nobody really cared. The black kids needed a school to go to, and so we all went to school together. I don't know if Borger, Texas, was any different from the rest of the South, but I can't remember anyone saying anything bad about the black kids going to what was an all-white school system. For the most part, everybody got along just fine, and some of the black kids did a lot for the sports programs at Borger High School and the junior high school as well.

Remembering back on my school years, I had gone to East Ward Grade School for the fourth, fifth, and half of the sixth grade. In the last half of the sixth grade, I went to Central Grade School because it was a lot closer. I had a Cushman Eagle motor scooter that I rode, and Central was a lot closer.

Sometimes, I wonder if I made a mistake by wanting to change things for whatever reason. I would sometimes change things when leaving it alone would have been much better in the long run. That is history now, and I don't have the power to change yesterday, let alone what I did fifty years ago.

My dad came home one day with this motor scooter in the back of his pickup truck. I think I remember he paid $125.00 for it. It was white. Ronny and I couldn't believe our eyes; it was ours. It didn't run very well, and dad had to have some work done on it to get it to start and run better. We changed the exhaust pipe from a single exhaust to two, one on each side, with no mufflers. It sounded great and also ran better. We had a blast riding this thing until, one day, the kickstand broke. We took it to a shop called Fuzzy's Radiator. Fuzzy had a welding machine and was going to fix the kickstand.

Well, Fuzzy fixed radiators and that was about all he was smart enough to do well, I think. He didn't notice there was a small amount of gas that had leaked out from somewhere and was on the floor under the scooter. When ol' Fuzzy struck the arc on the welder, the whole place was on fire in two seconds. The radiator shop and the scooter went up in flames that day and made the front page of the newspaper. I wouldn't have given two cents for the radiator shop, but my scooter was in there and was burnt to a crisp. The fire department was Johnny-on-the-spot and had the fire out before it burnt the entire building down, except for the part where my scooter was.

Dad had just spent about seventy dollars on getting my scooter running great, and now it looked like a crispy critter with handlebars. Fuzzy said, "Don't worry my insurance will fix everything, and you will get your scooter back just like brand new." Great, the only thing we didn't know was this was going to take almost a year to fix.

I was going into the eighth grade, and in Texas, you could get your driver's license at fourteen. I knew that at the end of the year, I could drive a car, and a motor scooter wouldn't haul girls as well as a car. Well, at the time, I didn't have either.

We finally got the scooter back in the late spring, almost a year after it burned up, and it really looked great. Fuzzy put in a new motor, new tires, new everything except the frame. It had new chrome dual exhausts, and the paint had no chips in it, and wow, it ran even better than a new Cushman Eagle.

The year that the scooter was in the shop was not cool at all because we either walked or had to be driven by our parents everywhere we went.

During the school year, I was in physical education, and one winter day, when the weather was very bad, we were in the gym messing around, and the coach wanted us to run. I had left my gym shoes at home, so I was running around the basketball court in my socks. As I came past the locker room, some guy stepped out from behind the locker room, and I didn't see him. We collided, and I tripped and hit the locker room wall with my left arm. More exactly, my left elbow. The coach looked at my arm and saw that my elbow was dislocated. I was taken to the hospital, where my elbow was not only dislocated but also broken in three places. The next eight weeks in a cast were not fun at all. I finally got the arm out of the cast, and Dr. Hammer told me to keep the arm in a sling for another week or so to get more movement into the elbow.

The same night, we went out to eat, and I didn't want to look uncool with the sling. So, I left it off and went into the café with my folks and brother to have dinner. No sooner had we sat down, someone came up from behind me that I did not see and flipped me on the ear. I turned around, and there stood Dr. Hammer. He said to me, "I thought I told you to wear the sling for another week." Well, what could I say? But the truth and that was I didn't want to look uncool. My elbow and ear recovered nicely that spring and have, for the most part, worked fairly well ever since.

My experience with boxing began as a result of Ronny having made an enemy of a kid named Wayne Jones. This kid was the typical bully type and picked on Ronny every chance he got. One day, as Ronny was coming home from school, this Jones kid came along and was giving Ronny a very hard time. When I showed up with a friend of mine, I had about enough of this little smart-ass kid, so I said to him, "If you want to pick on someone, try me." Well, the fight was on, and it only took about two minutes to kick his ass but good. It was a fair fight and I was just much better than Jones.

Not long after, we were in the gym at school. The coach wanted us to have boxing matches because it was raining, and we couldn't go outside for physical education. I fought a kid that almost every kid in the class was afraid of. This kid had a reputation of being Johnny badass and no one wanted to get in his way. We had on 16-ounce boxing gloves. You couldn't get hurt with them, so this kid was not going to have an easy time boxing with me. When we finished, the coach came over to me and said, "I have never seen any kid your size that had that hard a punch." He asked if I was left-handed. I told him I was right-handed and then he wanted to know why I fought lefty style. I didn't know; it just felt natural to do it that way.

This coach was also the Golden Gloves boxing coach and wanted me to get into boxing, which was not going to happen. I just didn't like it that well. But, not long after that, I was going to fight with the gloves on again.

This coach was a little different than most, I think, because he asked if I would fight in an outlaw match that paid twenty dollars. He said it would sort of be like a pro boxing outlaw fight. I asked whom I would fight, and ~~when~~ the coach said Wayne Jones. I said yes. The match was to be three rounds and the first match of the night on a ten-match card. I knocked out Jones in the first round with a left hook that sent him down for the count. They had to put smelling salts under his nose to get him up. We were using six-ounce gloves, and with them, I could hit very hard. A month later, this coach wanted to know if I wanted to fight again. I told him I would and asked who I would fight this time. It was the kid I fought in the gym. Well, this fight only lasted two rounds. With another big left hook, I sent Jimmy down for the count. Borger Texas had some very good boxers that had gone all the way to the state championships and some that were state champs. I was getting a reputation not as a good boxer but as a good fighter because these fights were not golden gloves. These were fights for money. The guy I fought on the street and in the first boxing match still didn't like Ronny and now didn't like me much either.

Not long after the second boxing match this Jones kid was coming past me just outside the side entrance to the school. I wasn't looking his way, and from out of nowhere, he tried to Sunday punch me. Well, I didn't go down as he thought I would, and the fight was on again. He thought he would win because he had the first punch in and was ready to finish me off. He swung with his right and I ducked and came up with a left that started at almost the ground, and I hit him just above the right eye. I hit him so hard that it gave him a concussion and sent him to the hospital. I won this fight as well, but I didn't come out very well in the end. I turned around and looked at my left hand, which was in a lot of pain, and saw that my index finger was dislocated. I wound up at the doctor's office, and from the x-rays, I had a broken knuckle and a broken finger. Well, that ended my boxing. The doctor said that I should not fight again because of the damage to my hand. That was fine with me because I didn't like it much anyway.

Borger had a radio station whose call letters were KBBB. In 1958, they had a program in the afternoon that had guest DJs for two hours. The guest DJs were kids from the Borger schools. I only lived two blocks from the radio station and I was one of the first selected to be a guest DJ. I was a little nervous. But I sat there next to the DJ, announced the songs, and talked to the kids who called in requests for their favorite songs to be played on the radio. I did this for a whole week, and it was a blast. I got very popular in school that week because I did a pretty good job as a DJ. But at the end of the week, my career in radio ended, and I didn't go any further with it.

This was just a couple of months before I got a license to drive a car, not just ride a little scooter with a Kick-starter and dual chrome exhausts. Driving a car, now that was going to be so cool. Women, more women, and being able to go further than ten miles away from the house.

At the end of the school year, I signed up for driver's education, summer school. It lasted only six weeks, and the car we used for Drivers Ed was unique, to say the least. The regular car was not available for summer school. So, the school borrowed the Driver's Ed teacher's car and had a brake pedal installed on the passenger's side. The car was a 1957 Ford two-door hardtop with a full continental kit on the back. It was red and black and looked like anything but a Driver's Ed car.

After finishing the six-week school, I went down to take my driving test for a driver's license in my parent's car. The car was a 1956 Lincoln Town Car. It was longer than the '57 Ford with the continental kit on it.

It was also my birthday, July 9, 1959, and I was going to have a driver's license on my birthday. I passed and did very well, even on the parallel parking. I took the car back home so my mother could go shopping and she told me my dad wanted to see me. I asked where he was, and my mother said she thought he was downtown. I asked her if she would take me to where my dad was. She told me she was busy and that if I needed to get to town right now, I should walk.

I headed to town walking and found my dad about thirty minutes later, on Main Street at a garage. He was talking with a policeman about something, and as I walked up, he introduced me to the cop. We stood around there for a while, and my dad came over to where I was looking at a car. He asked, "How do you like that car, son."

"Fine," I said, "Why do you ask?"

"Well," he said, "I just bought this car from the policeman I was talking to."

Dad gave the car to me for my birthday. Wow, I now have a driver's license and a new car all in one day.

The car was a 1950 Ford Club Coupe, burgundy with rolled and pleated upholstery. It had a stick shift, but on the steering column, and a flathead V8. You knew you were a driver when you could drive down the street with your arm around a girl drinking a coke and shifting the gears on the column at the same time. I could and did, and it was cool.

In the late 1950's with Elvis and blue suede shoes, being cool was important. I was no different than any other kid in the Texas Panhandle. No one wanted to be very different from anybody else.

One of the kids up the street, whose father was the used car manager at the Chevrolet dealership, saw my new '50 Ford and didn't speak to me for a week. I didn't let that bother me because it was his sister I wanted to be friends with anyway. The kid up the street was Mike Hanner, and he never rode in my '50 Ford. He was Chevrolet to the bone, and he even got mad at his sister Diann for riding in the Ford with me. Mike later went on to marry a very wealthy girl from west-central Texas and was given a car dealership for a wedding present. He later pooped all that off and wound up not doing very well. His dad and little brother bought two car dealerships just out of Abilene, Texas, that they still own to this day.

I dated their sister Diann on and off for a couple of years, and she wound up marrying a guy from Perryton, Texas and has lived in Tulsa for many years.

I kept the '50 Ford the next year and drove it to high school in the fall and spring of 1960. One morning, the neighbor from up the street brought a very unusual Chevrolet home with him, and I thought it looked like the wildest car I had ever seen. This was number thirteen of sixteen El Morocco Chevrolets, a very rare and very expensive car, especially if I still owned it today. All four of us kids took this car to Amarillo that morning, and when we got downtown, we stopped at a service station at 10th and Tyler. We paid a kid nine dollars to wax the car, and then we drove it to the Tri-State Fair Grounds for a car show. This El Morocco Chevrolet was completely stock from the factory in every way but took first place in radical custom.

In the late fall of 1958, my dad, along with many others, got laid off from Phillips. Mother was still teaching school at East Ward so it was not really bad for us. Dad bought a GMC truck from a guy in Kansas City, and just after the first of January 1959, I went with my dad to Kansas City to get it.

There was one interesting thing that happened while we were there. We were going downtown to get the title for the truck. The truck's owner was driving, and the place where we were to pick up the title was in the middle of a street in downtown KC. We had stopped to turn left into the parking lot and the car behind us started honking his horn. Now, the owner of the GMC truck was six foot eleven inches tall and not skinny either. He never said a word– just put the truck in park and got out. He walked back to the car behind us, leaned over to look in the window, said something to the driver, and calmly walked back to the car and got in. We turned into the parking lot, and he said to my dad, "I very nicely explained to that SOB that if he honked his horn again, I would rip out the horn and shove it up his ass." I think he got the message.

We drove back to Borger in the worst snowstorm since '57. It took us eight hours longer to get home because of the snow.

That year, my dad hauled gravel for roads in the Panhandle. In the summer of that year, he was helping build a new highway from Perryton to Pampa. The gravel pit was in the canyons just north of the Canadian River. One day, I asked if I could go with him and go hunting in the canyons. We got to the pit around seven thirty that morning, and I watched some of the trucks being loaded. Then I started walking into the canyons with my 20-gauge shotgun.

I was about two miles from the gravel pit and almost to the bottom of the canyon when I heard a very strange sound coming from behind me and to the left. I had just come around this big rock that was about twenty feet tall. I was maybe ten yards away from it and I quickly turned toward the sound. It sounded like a deep growl and the hair stood up on the back of my neck. As I looked up to the top of the rock, there sat a mountain lion. Just as I looked up at him, the lion stood up, and I shot very quickly. I didn't look to see if I had hit him. I just took off as fast as I could run, loading another shell into the chamber of the shotgun. I stopped and looked back at the rock, not knowing where the lion was. I started walking back toward the rock very slowly with the gun ready to shoot. No lion was to be seen as I came up to the rock.

Now I was starting to get very nervous because I didn't know if I had killed the lion or just wounded the big cat. I'm sure I was shaking all over and was taking very small steps as I began to look around the side of the big rock. I heard a sound like someone trying to blow his nose, then a growl of sorts. I stepped back and looked up to the top of the rock, and there was the lion standing at the edge, looking down at me with blood coming from his nose and mouth, and eyes. I didn't know it at the time but the shot from the 20-gauge had hit the lion in both eyes, and I'm sure he could not see me. He could hear me, but I guess, being blind, he just stood there, not knowing what to do. I didn't give him a chance to decide either. I shot again, this time with better aim and at very close range with the number 4 shot. The whole load of shots hit the lion in the neck and side of the head. He went down with a thud and slid off the rock not fifteen feet in front of me. I loaded another shell in the gun and slowly walked over to the lion and saw that he was dead. I don't know just how long I stood there staring at him, but when I decided to go, I took off in a hurry. I headed back to the gravel pit to tell someone that I had just shot a mountain lion. My dad and I walked back to see this large cat that I had bagged, and in all the excitement, I couldn't find the rock and couldn't find the big cat either. All I got out of it was one heck of a story.

ᓚᔐChapter Four᠙᠍᠍

Every September in Amarillo, Texas, the Tri-State Fair is held for ten days. It is an event most people in the Panhandle of Texas look forward to each year. As a kid growing up in that part of the world, it meant a huge carnival with lots of people, rides, food, and sideshows. It meant the end of summer and the start of colder weather, going back to school and seeing all the kids you didn't see throughout the summer.

The fall of 1959 was no different. We all went to ride the rides and eat stuff like cotton candy, corn dogs, and all the junk we didn't see all the time in Borger, Texas. We all loaded up in the car and headed to Amarillo to the Fair. The next year would be an election year, and we would have a new President in the United States. Eisenhower had been the President for the last eight years, and it looked like it would be a race between the Vice President, Richard Nixon, and John Kennedy, a senator from back east somewhere.

As we arrived at the Fair and were walking into the fairgrounds there was a large crowd gathered in front of one of the buildings. My dad and I walked over to where all these people were, and on the stage was the Vice President of the United States of America giving a speech. This was the first time I had ever seen a Vice President in person, and I wanted to get as close as we could. We were off to the side of the stage where most of the news people were standing. The speech came to an end, and Richard Nixon started down the steps of the stage, where all the reporters were standing. What happened next is something I have wondered about for the last fifty years.

Richard Nixon, the Vice President of the United States of America, walked right past all the reporters and walked up to my dad and stuck out his hand to him and said, "Hello Arlie, it's been a long time, and how have you been." Dad told him fine and then introduced me to the Vice President.

I never found out about that meeting and how my dad knew Nixon, but I think there were many things about my dad I wish I knew more about. Dad was a great father to us boys and, for the most part, a good husband, but there were many things about his past he would not ever talk about.

The spring of 1960 in Borger, Texas, was one of the wildest three months one could go through while in high school. It all started with a trial on television in Amarillo, Texas.

This trial was for the owner of an army surplus store charged with blowing up a restaurant in Amarillo with dynamite. Why this would happen because the owner of the army surplus store also had most of the cigarette machines in the Amarillo area. When someone else tried to put in a machine in a business, the owner of the business was told he should only use their machines, or else and they would decline the offer from the new company. If it sounded like the Mafia, you are right. It was, and right out of Chicago. Well, this trial was on TV every day, and everyone in the Panhandle of Texas watched it daily. No one wanted to believe the mob had such a hold on businesses in the area.

I'm not sure if the events on TV started all that happened in Borger with the high school kids or not, but I think it helped. The kids in high school started stealing everything they could get their hands on. Ripping off stores for clothing, booze, candy, and just about anything not nailed down. The cops were at the school every day for a month, taking kids in to be questioned and to jail. Now, this was not the kids from across the tracks; this was the sons and daughters of the preachers, doctors, lawyers, teachers, judges, and most of the high-class kids in school. These kids were being taken to jail by the dozens every day. One of the school principal's sons was arrested for running a casino in his basement.

One morning, as I parked my car in the parking lot at the school, there was a bunch of guys standing behind a car with the trunk open. They were putting guns in the trunk of another car that had its trunk open and where the guns were being taken out.

Just as school started that morning, four or five police cars drove up to the front of the school, and most of the guys who were moving the guns were taken to the police station. I'm not sure what they would have done, but since they all got arrested, it didn't happen. I heard that afternoon they were planning to take over the school.

Three guys stole a beer truck and had a party for the whole school with free beer for all in attendance. There were prostitutes during those two months that before were cheerleaders for the football team. It was crazy, stupid, and just plain nuts in the high school that spring. The result was a lot of kids wound up with records and probation for years, and all I got was a fat lip.

One kid saw me talking to a police officer one day and thought I must be telling the other kids about what was going on at the school. Actually, it was the guy my dad bought the car from, the '50 Ford Club Coupe. He was giving me some of the paperwork for the car. A kid named Bobby got mad and wanted to fight, so that day after school, we did. Bobby was six feet five, and I was only five feet eight, so the fight was not one I wanted to get into. But fight we did. I hit him, and he hit me in the lip, which bled a little, and somebody yelled out the cops are coming. The next thing me, and Bobby were running alongside each other to get the hell out of there.

My mother got very upset because, as a teacher, she was hearing all kinds of things going on at the high school that I didn't hear. One of the rumors the teachers were hearing was somebody was going to get killed for telling on the other kids, and this made my mother very nervous.

To make a long story short, she pulled me out of school. Since we were going to move to Spearman after school was out anyway, I spent the last month of school not attending and working on my cousin's farm in Spearman.

In June, we moved to Spearman, and I cut wheat all summer and then started school again in the fall at Spearman High.

That summer, every time it rained, Ronny and I would go swimming at the pool in Spearman. By the middle of August, we had met a lot of high school kids. Most of the guys were talking about playing football for the high school team. Ronny and I had never played on a school team. In Borger, for some reason, we just didn't go out for sports. I guess, looking back, we did too many other things and didn't want to use up all our free time playing football or basketball. However, I was on the Golf team in the eighth and ninth grades.

My dad had gotten a set of clubs for Christmas in 1957 and he only played with them two or three times that I can remember. I kind of took them over and played almost every day till we moved to Spearman in 1960.

It was August, and the wheat was all cut. We were back in Spearman getting ready to start football practice in a week or so when one of the guys we had met asked us if we wanted to go camping with the Explorer Scouts. The reason they wanted us is we had a pickup truck.

This trip was different, to say the least. There were nine of us guys and one dad. We left Spearman in two pickups with three guys in the bed of each truck and the rest in the seat. Each of us took turns riding in the back of the pickups. We were headed to the mountains in Colorado north of Denver, in Rocky Mountain National Park.

We had sleeping bags, tents, tarps, and all our gear in the beds along with three guys riding in each. The guys told us to bring all our cowboy stuff with us as we were going to help a rancher move his cows down from the high pastures while we were there. Part of the Scout thing, I guess.

We arrived in the mountains and set up camp at the edge of a National Park campground somewhere west of Estes Park, about eight miles west, as I remember. We had six tents that were small but big enough for two guys to sleep in and one for keeping all our food and other things in. We cooked over a campfire and sat around the fire telling stories and did a few other things at night that almost got us kicked out of the National Park for life.

Each day, we would go to the Johnson Ranch, saddle up horses, and help move cows down from the high pastures. It was a blast doing that because Ronny and I were not real cowboys. We faked it so well that no one ever knew that. We were kids from the panhandle of Texas, and we knew enough to watch the real cowboys and do everything they did. It worked like a charm. Each day we would be back at the ranch with the cows by noon and would then take the horses and just ride the mountains in the afternoon.

One day, we rode to the top of Lookout Mountain and back. This is above the tree line and had a watchtower for forest fires at the very top. The rangers at the bottom usually hauled up supplies by mule each week. They saw us starting to go up and asked if we would carry the supplies up for them.

"Not a problem," we said, and when we got to the top, the rangers treated us like kings. They gave us a tour of the fire tower and fixed us sandwiches for lunch.

That night, we had fried chicken for dinner. While cooking the chickens, we noticed one of them had a bad smell, so we didn't cut it up or put it into the frying pan. After dinner my brother and another guy took small green tree limbs and inserted them into the legs and wings of the chicken, so he was doing the spread eagle, then put a small twig into his neck and a potato for a head. A small carved stick was used for a beak then we rolled the chicken in the coals of the campfire until the yard bird was black. As you might think, this was an awful-looking bird or monster or whatever.

We, that is, the whole group of us, took this monster and hung it from the ceiling of the women's outhouse in the campground, then hid behind rocks up the mountain. It was not going to be a long wait for here came two women up the hill to use the bathroom. This was going to be fun.

The two women opened the door and shined their flashlights into the darkness of the outhouse. Well, not only was the bird suspended from the ceiling, but it was also attached to the door, so when it opened, the monster moved forward as if wanting to fly out the door.

I have heard screaming before, but not like that. When the door was opened, and our creation started moving forward in only the light from the flashlight, I'm sure it looked very, very scary, to say the least. Well, as I said, these two ladies screamed and started running down the hill into the campground. In the meantime, Ronny and one of the other guys went to the door and removed the monster and back up the hill behind the rocks they went in a hurry.

None too soon either, because within three minutes, here came the husbands of the ladies followed by the women and a park ranger. This was going to be very funny. When the two men opened the door and looked in and saw nothing, they just looked at each other and started laughing. We could hear them talking but not what they were saying as the men started back down the hill with the ladies and the park ranger in tow. The women were not going to let anything be nothing and kept saying that there was indeed a monster in the outhouse.

This was our chance, and we didn't pass it up. We put the creature back in the outhouse. The women were going to get the last word and then decided that no one was going to listen to them and remembered that they still needed to go potty. After following the men back down the hill, they gave up, and here they came again.

Now the women knew the outhouse was clear of monsters, so they had no fear and walked straight to the bathroom door and, with a jerk, opened the door. Here it came again, this time almost hitting the first woman in the face. I have heard screaming before, but not like that, and this brought the men and the park ranger running. The only thing we could do at this time was to stay hidden behind the rocks and try not to laugh so loud as to give away our position.

The park ranger, I think, knew instantly who was responsible for this practical joke and was not going to let it go without a warning as to our actions.

The next morning, while having breakfast, the ranger showed up at our camp. He could hardly keep a straight face while giving us a stern tongue-lashing about the chicken in the outhouse. We did all we could to keep from laughing about it also.

This turned out to be just one event in a day full of the unusual. Before the ranger showed up at our camp, we had another visitor that caused some commotion. Ronny and the other guy in their tent were still sleeping when they heard a low growl, and when they opened the tent flap, they were eye-to-eye with a mountain lion. We believed they scarred each other, and the lion made a hasty retreat back into the hills. I guess throwing the tent flap and hitting the lion in the face, which I'm sure the lion didn't expect, spoiled the lion's desire to find something in our camp for breakfast.

By the time we were finished with our breakfast it started raining lightly and didn't let up as we headed for the ranch to saddle up and get started bringing down the cattle to the lower pastures. The ranch foreman told us the rest of the hands had other things to do that day and that we could take the horses and go where we wanted. We decided we would ride into the town down the mountain, which was about seven miles.

We each had a yellow rain parka in our saddlebags which we all put on as we started out down the side of the road into town. About an hour into the trip, a truck stopped, and two guys got out and waved at us to stop. They told us they were with a company that shot film for newsreels for the movies. They told us we looked like the James Gang from a hundred years ago and asked if they could film us as we rode along the road into town. We said sure, and the guys got their cameras out of the truck and did just that. They followed us for a mile or more in the mist and rain and low clouds. They told us thanks, said goodbye, and told us to look for this in the movies in the next month or two. Sure enough, we made the big screen in October 1960 and were shown for about a month in movie theaters across the country. That is my only time as a movie star, but not the end of being on TV.

We all had a great time on that trip, and when we returned to Spearman, it was time to start football practice. All the guys we had met that summer played football and wanted to know if Ronny and I were going to go out for the team. Sure, we told them we wanted to play and be a part of anything in the schools to help with the transition from Borger to Spearman.

We were making new friends and a new start in a new town, and we were very interested in all that was going on there.

Football practice started two weeks before school started, and this was the end of August. We got all our football gear with helmets, shoulder pads, and everything else we needed to look like football players. We went from the locker room to the practice field with great expectations of gridiron. We got to the practice field and started warming up. Across the street to the east of the football field were some cattle pens, cattle, and cowboys. Now, these cowboys were branding these cattle, and there was a slight breeze coming from the east.

We were running and getting hot and running some more and getting hotter, and now we started to smell the branding of the cattle. The burning hair and the sweat from running around the football field started to make us sick.

Well, it got bad. There were forty guys in football suits down on their knees with their helmets off, throwing up everything, and yes, I mean everything. Sick and tired was the theme of the day; maybe that is where the expression came from.

Well, the next few days, we were very sore, and it was only one week to the first game. Quite a number of the guys on the team had never played football before, and it was going to take a lot to become a good team. We were all on the B team, and the next Friday night, we played a scrimmage with Stinnett Texas, all of us, the varsity and the B team combined. Stinnett was smaller than Spearman, so we figured this would be easy. Well, it wasn't so easy after all because Stinnett had some things I didn't count on. Not playing football the years before, I didn't know much about the kids from any of the smaller towns in the Panhandle. I learned a lot over the next couple of weeks.

The first thing was I had never heard of Donny Anderson from Stinnett or his teammates. Even though I was on the B team, I started as left safety on defense. It was my first real football game in a football suit and a stadium with people in it.

We kicked off to Stinnett, and Donny Anderson ran over me and returned the ball to our forty-yard line. The first play of the game and Anderson got the ball and went forty yards for a touchdown. This continued the whole game. Give the ball to Donny and the ref would hold up both arms and blow his whistle with another six points for Stinnett. Donny Anderson is the one and the same that in the state track championships, won five first-place medals. He was six feet two inches and 220 pounds. He is also the one who got the Heisman three years later from Texas Tech University and went on to play for the Green Bay Packers and Kansas City Chiefs. On the same team, four other guys went on to play football in the NFL.

I saw Donny coming around the right end on one play, and I don't think he saw me coming at him as fast as I could run, which was fairly fast. I hit him about the waist, and both of us went out of bounds. As we got up Anderson patted me on the top of my helmet and said that was a nice tackle. Well, it was a little but not a lot because they wound up beating us by the score of fifty-one to nothing.

The second scrimmage game was played in Spearman the next Friday night after it had rained for two days and nights. The football field was nearly underwater, and by the end of the first quarter, there was water and mud more than there was grass on the field.

I started on defense again as a safety, even though on the B team, I started as a running back on offense.

On one play, Borger's quarterback threw a pass that I intercepted, and I took off down the sideline. When I got hit by one of the Borger players, we both slid out of bounds underwater, and I mean underwater. I thought I was going to drown for a second or two. I had so much mud in my facemask that I had to take the helmet off to get all the mud out.

Borger kicked our butts worse than Stinnett did. This was not a very good start to my football career.

By the third game of the year, I was just starting to become a football player. I had two practice games and two regular season games on the B team under my belt and playing was getting easier. I was a starting running back, and by the end of the second game, starting to do things right, that is, making good yardage on some plays and finding the holes in the defense.

The third game was against Stratford at Stratford. The varsity coach was at the game to watch; I think he was looking for up-and-coming talent for the varsity team. In the first half of the game, I really started getting this football thing right. I had run for over a hundred yards and had scored two touchdowns rushing. During the half, the varsity coach came over to me and said that if I did the same thing in the second half, I would start as a running back on the varsity team the next night. Wow, I thought that would be great and wanted to play as hard as I could to impress him even further in the second half.

By the end of the third quarter, I was doing just that, making one first down after another and on three plays in a row, running for over fifty yards. That drive started on our ten-yard line, and in three plays, we were on Stratford's thirty-eight-yard line. I got the call for the fourth time in a row and went off tackle and through the secondary for another fifteen-yard gain. I was tackled by one of the safeties, and his knee came down on my right shoulder as I hit the ground. With the ball under my right arm and this guy's knee on my shoulder, it was a very bad way to end my football career. The bone in my upper arm snapped off with a sound that was like a gun going off. I was helped to the sidelines and sat there on the bench for a couple of seconds.

I tried to move my right arm, and it wouldn't do anything. I have had some experience with parts of my body being broken, and I knew this was bad. I told the coach that I thought my shoulder was broken and that I needed to go to the hospital.

I was taken to the hospital in Spearman because Stratford didn't have one. When I got there, the Doctor took x-rays of my arm. When he came back into the room, he said he had never seen a break like that, and I would need to go to the hospital in Amarillo to get it fixed.

At the Amarillo hospital, the doctors that looked at the x-rays were a little confused because they had not seen many like it. The ball at the top of my arm bone was broken in half, and it was down beside the arm bone. They said maybe it could be fixed by just moving the top half of the ball back into place and doing it without cutting my shoulder. They did but it took over five hours in the operating room. They put me in sort of a cast from my waist up around my neck and right arm. Ten weeks in that mess was a long time to heal up. It did, and they got it within sixteen one-thousandth of an inch-perfect. It still works today and pretty well, too.

That ended my football career in high school, but there were other sports and girls. I only thought there were other sports at Spearman High, well, not for me. One day, most of the football players were engaged in wrestling matches, and I was doing very well. I beat three guys in a row when the assistant football coach came over to me and asked why I was working out with the football team. He said, "With your shoulder as it is, we have decided not to let you go out for the team next year."

I got very angry and did something that I have done far too often in my life. I wanted to change everything, and right now. It was just at the end of the semester and I wanted to find another school to go to.

Ronny and I drove over to Morse that Saturday to look around. We or my dad had just leased a farm thirteen miles south of Spearman and we were moving into the farmhouse there.

Morse was only nine miles from the farm and would be closer. Good logic, and I had a reason, remember? Morse is and was a very small town. Like two hundred people in the whole town, but a lot of farms around with lots of kids, we thought. We stopped in front of the school to take a look when a new Cadillac came down the street in front of the school, going at least seventy miles per hour. Just before you get to the school to the south, there is a dip in the road. It's not just a little dip but a real dip. The Cadillac didn't slow down even five miles per hour, and when it went through the dip, all four wheels came off the ground. The girl driving the Caddy never let off the gas either. I looked at Ronny and told him this must be pretty cool, and the girl was good-looking as well. She waved at us as the Caddy hit the ground again, and the sparks flew from underneath the car. To make a long story short we both transferred to Morse High School the next week.

We really wanted to make an impression on everyone when we started school at Morse, so on the first day, we both wore Spearman football jackets. I guess no one really cared because by the end of the first week, we knew everyone in the school, and I think we were very well-liked. We didn't know the school was having some problems. Some of the parents wanted to move their kids to other schools and split up the school district. They wanted to end the High School and just have a grade school. Well, as it turned out, the next year was the last year Morse had a high school. But some of the things that happened that year are worth telling about.

It was in late March when the school board had a community meeting to discuss splitting up the high school. Ronny and I really liked the school and were doing well in our studies. This was very important to Ronny because he didn't do well with his studies. Ronny liked the small classes and the teachers having enough time to work with each person. This really helped Ronny. So, my dad went to the school board meeting to express his thoughts about this good school.

I guess the meeting was going well, with tempers almost to the boiling point, when there was a commotion in the parking lot. Everyone quit hollering at each other to see what was going on outside.

When all the men came outside to see what was going on, I was standing in the middle of the parking lot holding a double-barrel 12-gauge shotgun and looking very mean at Allen Dixon. Allen was saying the school should be moved, and I shot him with both barrels at once.

Now, when the gun went off, Ronny, who was behind the first car behind Allen, jerked the rope he was holding that was around Allen's waist. The shotgun was loaded with blanks, and Allen was holding a hand full of catsup, which he slapped on his chest as Ronny jerked the rope. Ronny was very strong and pulled a little bit too hard because Allen landed on the hood of the car. It was all a show to let these grown men see how silly they were being about all this.

It brought the meeting to a halt, and after Allen recovered somewhat, Ronny, Allen, and I all lined up and took a bow with smiles on our faces.

As strange as it was, no one ever said a word to any of us about what we did that night, but it stopped all the bickering about the school. They decided to settle where the kids would go to school a little more peacefully.

The next year, which turned out to be next to the last for Morse High School, the school was a little smaller, but Ronny and I still liked it a lot. We got to know everyone during the rest of the year. When school was out, we had made a lot of friends at Morse.

My dad had rented a farm at the first of the year, thirteen miles south of Spearman, Texas. After much cleaning of the farmhouse, we moved from town to the farm. It was great living in the country and doing all the things I loved doing, like hunting rabbits and the like. Working on the farm was fine for me and Ronny. We had a lot of great times the first year plowing and changing irrigation water with tubes.

They don't do much of that nowadays, as most farmers use sprinkler systems. We ran the water down a ditch and had two-inch tubes that had to be set in the rows to make the water run down the rows. Setting irrigation tubes is now a lost art, but I was good at it. I could set them as fast as I could walk. Ronny would move the tubes from the last day, and I would start them again in the new rows.

One day that summer, I was at the irrigation well checking on the tubes when Ronny and a friend drove up to see if I needed any help. There was a storm cloud building to the southwest and it was starting to sprinkle rain. Ronny was driving a VW beetle, and because I had on rubber irrigation boots that were very muddy, Ronny popped the trunk lid. I sat on the bumper to get out of the rain so I could still talk to them without getting wet.

The next thing I remember was Ronny and his friend picking me up out of the ditch and asking me if I was all right. I told them I thought I was, and the last thing I remembered was hearing the thunder and a loud pop when the lightning hit. I think because I was wearing rubber boots, they kept the lightning from killing me. It knocked me about ten feet over into the bar ditch and out cold for a few seconds. Other than being a little nervous over how close that was, I had no ill effects from the lightning.

Summer was cutting wheat and plowing and cutting wheat and plowing. We took our combine to Floydada, Texas, to cut wheat before ours was ready. This was in late May, and the further south you go, the earlier the wheat is going to be ready to cut. We parked next to another single combine crew and, after talking with them for a while, decided to work together because more farmers wanted two machines rather than one.

A farmer who also owned a grain elevator came up to where we were parked and asked who was running this outfit. One of the hands told him it was the guy working on the combine and pointed at me. The farmer whose name was Jay North, couldn't believe that a sixteen-year-old was running this outfit. But, after talking with me about his wheat and us driving out to look at his fields, I think he was convinced that I knew what I was doing. We agreed on the price and moved our machines to his wheat field and unloaded them. The next morning, we started cutting his wheat, and I could see it was not as ready as the farmer stated the day before. There was a lot of wet or green wheat on one side of his wheat field. We moved to another side of the field, and the wheat was a lot drier. The farmer drove up and asked why we had moved to the other side. I told him where we were; at the wheat was wet, and this side of the field was more ready to cut. We had two trucks loaded and were taking them to the elevator when the weather started to change with a few sprinkles. The rain then started falling, and we shut down the machines and went back to town. It rained just enough to stop us from cutting for a couple of days, so we headed back to Spearman.

When we got back and started cutting the farmer's wheat again, it was riper now, and we would get into high gear on his fields. We had cut all morning and had four to five loads delivered to his elevator when he drove up again and wanted to talk to me. I was driving the combine so he had to wait for me

45

to get to the end of the field. As I was unloading the grain into the truck Mr. North said he was not going to pay what we already had agreed on. I couldn't believe what he was telling me and at sixteen years old I didn't want to argue with him. So, I told him I would call my dad and Mr. North just got in his pickup truck and drove away.

I shut my machine down and took the now-loaded truck to the elevator myself. I told my hired hand to stay there and look like he was working on the combine if Mr. North came back.

I called my dad from the grain elevator and told him what the farmer said about the price for cutting the wheat. My dad said to shut the machine down and he would be there as fast as he could. It was about two hundred miles from Spearman, but my dad was there in less than three hours. When he got there, the farmer showed up again, and I couldn't hear all that was said, but the farmer left in a hurry, and my dad was very hot under the collar.

He told us to get the combine back to town and not cut another grain of wheat for this son-of-a-gun. We drove back into Floydada and spent the night. The next morning, my dad called me and asked if I could drive the combine all the way back to our farm rather than load it on the truck to haul it back.

"Sure," I said. I was sixteen and could do just about anything.

Well, the next morning before the sun came up, we headed for Spearman, at all of twelve miles per hour, as that was as fast as the combine would run. About ten o'clock, we came to the Palo Duro Canyon. This was something I hadn't thought about when I said I could drive the combine home. That canyon is ten miles across and two thousand feet deep, or so it seemed at the time. I started down the thing, and the only thought I had was not to hit the brakes, just drive the thing, and it would be ok. The road was very steep and had a lot of curves, but I could drive, and I kept my cool. This monster was fourteen feet wide and was now going about thirty miles per hour. I knew that if I hit the brakes, I would be in deep poo-poo very fast, so I just let her go and kept it between the ditches or between the rock wall and the cliff.

A combine steers with the rear wheels, not the front wheels, like most other vehicles. The slightest turn of the wheel causes the front end of the combine to move a lot. Also, to go around these curves, which were very tight and narrow, one had to be very smooth, and the first mistake would be my last mistake. Added to that, most of the weight is on the front of a combine and using the brakes was out of the question. I thought that on a couple of the curves if a car was coming toward me, I, as well as them, would be in a lot of trouble. I think I also got very lucky that no one was headed up the hill that morning.

When I got to the bottom, I stopped. A sheriff's car came up behind me and stopped also. The deputy walked up to me and said, "You did one hell of a job driving that thing just now.

"I just smiled and said, I guess you are right because I got it to the bottom just fine." That's when he told me that in the last two years, three men had been killed trying to do what I just did. I thought he was just kidding me until he started giving me the stories about how they died trying what I had successfully done. As it turned out it seems that I am the only person to ever drive a combine with the header on it across the Palo Duro Canyon and live to tell about it. The gear I used going down the hill is called Mexican Overdrive, or neutral.

Most of the summer in the Texas panhandle was spent working on the farm and hunting rabbits and just having fun. In August we were watering milo. My dad wasn't sure the water would go all the way through mile-long rows, so he cut a ditch in the middle of the field to bring more water to the east half of the milo. As it turned out the water would go all the way through and we had a ditch that wasn't needed. Dad told Ronny and me that if we would fix the ditch, we could go to Red River, New Mexico, when we finished. We took a tractor with a blade and smoothed the ditch out. But the only way water would go all the way to the end of the field was to hand-dig furrows in each row all the way across the field. We wanted to go to Red River, so at about five in the morning, we started digging. We took shovels and made furrows in each row all the way across this milo field. Each row needed about fifteen feet of digging, and there were about 300 rows in the field. This was work and I mean not easy work. We scooped dirt until about eight that evening and all the next day until we finished. Our dad was amazed that we did this job in such a short time. He didn't know just how much we wanted to go to Red River.

We went into town that evening, met up with Jimmy Stumpf, and started planning our trip to New Mexico. Our mother and dad said we could leave the next morning. So, we told our folks that we would spend the night with Jimmy and would go from there. Jimmy told his folks we would spend the night at our house and leave in the morning. At about eleven that evening, we were on our way to the mountains of New Mexico. We drove all night and got to Red River at about five in the morning. We stopped in a little valley, threw towels on the grass, and went to sleep for a few hours.

We didn't have much money, any of us, and the money we had was going to be used very wisely—girls and fun. Buying gas for the car just plain cost too much, and in that part of the country, at all hours of the night, there were no gas stations open anyway. That wasn't really a problem for three resourceful guys on our way to the mountains. We had an Oklahoma credit card and knew how to use it. The first small tractor we saw from the road ran on gas, and we borrowed ten gallons of this farmer's gas and left him an IOU, not signed, of course. When we arrived in Red River, we were low on gas again. This nice man had parked his Jeep with two five-gallon cans on the back, so we borrowed ten more gallons and left this nice fellow an IOU, unsigned, of course. This was working out fine, and we wouldn't need any more go juice until we were on our way home. We hadn't spent a single dime, and we had gone 350 miles to Red River. There was going to be lots of fun and girls for the next three days. If you don't know what an Oklahoma credit card is, I shall explain how it works. It is a four-foot section of garden hose and a five-gallon gas can.

We had a great time and hated to go back to the flatlands and back to work, but you gotta do what you gotta do. So back to Texas, we went with new girlfriends in Amarillo, Floydada, and Canyon, Texas. We went into the Village Inn Café for breakfast one morning. Before we left there, I was a little bit worried we might get killed by this guy who parked next to us.

Jimmy Stumpf was then, and still is to this day, a very good friend of mine. We have known each other for forty-eight years now, but Jimmy had a problem with his speech, and how it has kept from killing him many times, I don't know. He, out of the blue, will say the wrong thing at the wrong time and loud enough to be heard by the wrong people.

He said as we were going into this café to eat, "Would you look at that goofy little piece of crap car? It must be an idiot that drives that thing."

As we looked up, this guy about six feet six inches of him said, "That is my car, and what kind of idiot would drive that piece of crap you came up in."

Jimmy looked up at the very large fellow and said, "Well, this kind of idiot drives that piece of crap."

I thought we were going to be killed right then and there. Then they both started laughing at the same time, shook hands

49

and we went on about getting some bacon and eggs. How he gets away with some of the things he has said over the years I have never figured out. I guess I never will, for old Jimmy is still alive and well, living in North Carolina. We still talk to each other on the phone at least once a week to this day.

One day on the farm, the phone rang. My mother said the caller was her brother Paul Conway, and he was in the Panhandle and would like to come by the house for dinner. Mother told him to come right on. Paul then said he wanted to bring this fellow with him for he had promised the guy a real country down-home dinner on a farm in Texas. Mother said, "Come on, and we'll have fried chicken and all the fixins to go with it."

Paul and his friend showed up about an hour later, and the friend turned out to be Jock Michelin, the president of the Michelin tire company in Paris, France. Paul had lots of friends like that, for he traveled all over the world for Phillips Petroleum Company, selling rubber and many other things.

The rest of the summer, things went smoothly, and we made one more trip to Red River, me, Ronny, and Jimmy. We only stayed two days, and when we got home found a note from my Mother and Dad that they had gone to Red River for the weekend. It was raining in Spearman, so Jimmy could not work. So, we decided to go back to Red River ourselves. We only stayed in Spearman for about an hour, then headed back to New Mexico.

When we got back to Red River, we called the girls we had met the day before at a dance. We told them that if they really liked us, we would come back to Red River for the weekend. They said, "Yes, come on," and we drove to their motel and said hi. This was less than ten minutes later and they spent the rest of the day trying to figure out how we did that.

We had a very good time and finally told them we called from the Village Inn Café.

School started in September, summer was over, and it was my senior year. Morse was a very small school the year before and with some of the kids changing to other schools, it was even smaller now. There were three seniors, two juniors, and ten and fifteen in the ninth and tenth grades. This was to be the next to the last year of Morse High School. 1962 and I was one of three that were seniors. The next year, the graduating class would be even smaller, and the last one for Morse. The School started in 1917, and I was to be in the next to the last class to graduate from Morse. Now, it is only grades one through six and still not very big.

But here we were, seniors in high school and ready for all the things that seniors do. All three of us, me, Jack Gibblin, and Carolyn George. We had to have a class sponsor, a teacher. The one we chose was a new teacher named Angelia Ferguson, about twenty-four and good looking, to say the least. With this out of the way, we had elections, and I was named class president, editor of the annual staff, senior class favorite, most handsome, and captain of the basketball team. Within two weeks after school started, Jack and Carolyn started dating and about a year and a half later were married. Back to school...we had to build the school's annual book all by ourselves. We started having meetings after school to get this going. Now, as I stated, Jack and Carolyn became one within two weeks after the start of school, and these meetings were the four of us: Jack, Carolyn, Miss Ferguson, and me. Me, Angie Baby (Miss Teacher and twenty-four) got to be good friends rather quickly. One night, when we were having the annual staff meeting, Jack and Carolyn said they would go get some items we wanted for the annual, and they would be back in a few minutes. Angie had no idea where they were going and knew very little about the area. The items in question were about a twenty-five-mile round trip, and I knew they might stop on the way to smooch a little, so this was going to take an hour at least. That left me and Angie Baby there alone, in the house all by ourselves, and it was dark outside, and we were all alone.

I was a little nervous; Miss Ferguson was our teacher, twenty-four years old and very good-looking. I was seventeen and didn't have a clue what to do now. Angie sat down on the couch next to me and asked me to rub the back of her neck. I very nervously massaged her neck and shoulders for about five minutes. Miss Ferguson had a look on her face that pretty well said what she wanted me to do next. I was at least smart enough to see this as well. She put her hands on top of my hands that were on her shoulders and started pulling my hands down the front of her blouse to the tops of her breasts.

I very quickly said, "Is that Jack's car?" I stood up and walked to the front door to look out. I think she knew just how this would look and how scared to death I looked and decided to back off a little.

I knew I was a fairly good-looking guy, and I didn't have much problem attracting girls, but in 1961 screwing around with my English teacher didn't seem like the thing to do. She was much older looking, and I just wanted to be a high school senior. I did like the idea that this kind of woman thought I was cute or good-looking or handsome or whatever, and it did feed my ego a little.

At the end of September each year, the Tri-State Fair was held in Amarillo. We hardly ever missed a year going to the fair. Ronny and Allen Dixon said they wanted to go on Saturday, and I said I would go with them. Miss Ferguson overheard and said she had never been to the fair, and if we would like, she would take us all in her car. Ronny and Allen thought this was a great idea because none of our money would be spent on gasoline.

Well, we all met at Angelia's house and got into her car to go to Amarillo. Angie Baby said to me, "You know where we're going, so you drive." I got out of the car, walked around to the other side, and got in. She only moved over about a foot so that when I got behind the wheel, she was very close, and I mean very close. All the way to Amarillo she had her arm around my shoulders and with her right hand on my leg. I wasn't sure we were going to the fair or find a place to park somewhere on a lonely road and get my brains screwed out. We finally got to the parking lot at the fair. When Ronny and Allen got out, it was the last time I saw them for a couple of hours. They took off in a hurry to see all the sights at the fair.

That left me with Miss Ferguson, and she put her arm in mine, and we walked into the fairgrounds that way. Just inside the main gate was a Marine exhibit with three sharp-looking Marines in dress blues standing in front of their exhibit. The one in the middle was a very sharp-looking Marine sergeant. As we walked by, he took off his hat and said, "What in the hell does this guy have that we don't." I looked back at him and said, "Money and her." If looks could kill, I would be dead. I wish I could have heard all the rest of what he said, but the noise was very loud, and with all the people walking by, we just went on. Miss Ferguson looked to be in her mid-twenties and I looked all of seventeen and not a day more.

We walked around the fair, saw all the exhibits and the animals, and finally got to the midway, where all the rides were. As we were walking arm in arm, I'm sure there were many looks, such as the one from the Marine, but now I was starting to enjoy the attention we were getting.

We walked by the tunnel of love, and Angie Baby wanted to ride it, and I was dumb enough to say sure, let's go, and we did. We got into the car and started through the tunnel of love. It was dark and Angie put her hand on my leg, so I put my arm around her on the back of the chair of the car. As we continued on into the dark, her hand tightened on my leg, and I put my arm around her shoulders, and then we were kissing, tongue and all. I figured I was in this deep; I might as well give it all I had, and I put a kiss on her that she would not forget. I think that if we had enough time in the tunnel of love, I would have screwed my English teacher right there and then. We came out of the dark, still kissing and with her hand higher still on my leg and my hands all over her. She was hot, and I knew we had already gone too far, and I just wanted to get away from her for a few minutes or more.

What was I going to do now? We still had the one-hour drive back to Morse that night. I believe all Angie Baby wanted to do was screw a schoolboy that night.

I drove back to Morse as I had done on the way to Amarillo earlier in the evening. Angie was so close to me that if anyone looked it looked like we were one person in the car. Ronny and Alan dozed off on the way back, and Angie took full advantage of the situation. She was all over me on the drive back to Morse. It was all I could do to drive and kiss my teacher and play hands on the front of her body all the way back. I still wonder how we made it back to Morse without stopping and getting it on. Ronny and Alan slept all the way back, and I'm glad they were there. This would-be romance could have been really messy, for we would have probably stopped somewhere along the way, and I'm not really sure how this would have ended up.

Now, I had to figure out a way to end this before it got out of hand. I did all I could to stay away from Angelia for the next couple of weeks, and finally, one of the local guys in town asked her out, and they started going fairly steady. Was I glad and now I could get on with all that a senior does.

Over the next couple of months, we all went on ad-selling trips, but nothing happened to further this little romance.

I didn't do anything to encourage it, and Angelia kept her cool. I think the guy she had started dating was a big help.

We made it through the fall and into the winter of that senior year, and as I look back, it was a blast. Basketball season started, and I was captain of the team. We had as our Coach Jim Hensley, who the year before was known as Cotton Hensley, a defensive end for the Dallas Cowboys. At six feet eight and two eighty-five, he was a lot of coach. His only problem with our basketball team was the tallest player we had was Jack Gibblin, at six feet tall. I had no idea what was coming that year as far as basketball was concerned, but it was not long before I found out how much each team we played wanted to beat us.

The year before, the basketball team from Morse High School went undefeated the whole year. The team was made up of twin brothers at six feet eight and two guys at six-five and six feet six. The point guard was five foot eight. These five guys had played together all their lives and were very good, to say the least.

In the fall of 1961, when basketball season started, every team we played wanted revenge and got it. I think we only won one game the whole season.

In the early fall, my uncle and aunt from Muleshoe, Texas, came with their two boys to visit for the weekend. Saturday morning, our mothers and dads went into town and left us four boys doing our thing. We decided to hunt foxes in the pasture east of our house. The foxes had dug a lot of holes, and we needed to find a way to get them out of their holes. I had this idea that we could freeze them out by putting butane down the foxholes. Besides, we were sure they would not like the smell either. So, we injected about fifty gallons of butane, but no foxes. Then we got the idea that if they didn't like the cold butane, they might not like a lot of heat, so we got a five-gallon can of gasoline and put about half down a couple of the holes and set the holes on fire. Oh hell, this might work! Speaking of hell, fire and smoke were coming out of three of the four holes. We had used holes that were fifty or more feet from those we had put the butane into. I took the can of gas, went to another hole at the other end of the area, and thought if we started another fire, we would have all the foxes in the middle. Wrong, this did not work very well at all. As soon as I started pouring gas into the second hole, the can I was holding while pouring the gas exploded. It caught my shirt on fire and blew me about twenty feet backward into a dirt mound, thank God. I rolled over, and the soft dirt put the fire out. I was a little hot, to say the least. I had a blister on the left side of my chest and some blisters on my face and on my left arm. I would live to hunt again. The rest of that day, I was not sure I would live because it hurt like hell, and I thought my dad was going to cause me some more pain around my back side. I guess he figured I was in bad enough shape already, so he only gave a long and severe tongue-lashing.

Basketball practice on Monday was not fun either because of the blisters. When I went into the soft dirt, I also hit a cactus and had some of the needles in my left elbow, which was no fun at all.

I lived and played basketball all season, but this was not the only problem I would encounter. These were my stupid years, I guess because I would go to the emergency room at the hospital a few more times that year. My senior year was a real bummer in that I was in some kind of bandage for most of it.

In mid-December, I went to see my mother at her school, where she taught third grade. It had snowed about four inches and then cleared off and got very cold. When it got to nine below zero, they closed the school at Morse, so we got the day off. I went to Spearman and went by to see my mother, and she said it would be a few minutes before she was ready. So, I went into the gym and was shooting baskets. I had on cowboy boots, which is not really good on the basketball court, but that's what we wore all the time. I jumped to get a rebound and broke my right foot. Yes, the hospital was happy to see me again so soon after the foxfire. I was mostly healed up, and the blisters were just red spots on my side, and now I have a broken foot. You guessed it, I still played every game with a size nine on my left foot and a size eleven on the other one. We were getting our asses kicked every game anyway, so my being a little slower didn't seem to matter much.

That Friday night, it got down to twelve below zero, and the wind blew from the north about thirty miles per hour all night. About nine that evening, the phone rang, and it was the sheriff. He told my dad that someone had reported about thirty head of steers were on the highway and the snow was blowing so bad you could not see them until you were right on top of them. Dad asked me if I thought I could get them back in the pasture they came from with a pickup truck. I told him I didn't think so, but we could try. The cattle probably came from the place across the highway from us. He agreed and also didn't think a pickup truck would work to get thirty head of steers moved in that storm. My dear ol' dad then made an executive decision and said I should try to get the steers in using a horse.

I put on two pairs of Levis over long handles with three shirts, a sweatshirt, and a coat. Two pairs of gloves and tied a bath towel on my head. I looked like Nanook of the north, could hardly walk, and was very glad no one saw me dressed like this. Out to the barn, I went with saddle in hand. The horse, when he saw me, had a look on his face like, "You have got to be kidding." I put the saddle on the horse, and I wondered how I was going to get my leg bent enough to put my foot into the stirrup. I got on the horse and started out of the barn, and then the thirty-mile-per-hour wind hit us. I thought the horse was going on strike right then and there. My god, it was cold, and the quarter-mile ride to the highway made me think about the cowboys a hundred years ago and wonder how they made it. I think that might be why the life of the average man was only about forty-five years a hundred years ago.

I made it to the road, and sure enough, there were about thirty head of steers on the pavement. It was one of the only places where the wind had blown all the snow away. I saw lights from a pickup truck coming from our house, and Dad and my brother stopped at the corner and opened the gate to the pasture the steers came from. I got the steers moving in the right direction, and in a few minutes, we had them all back home in their pasture and off the road.

The ride back to the barn was against the wind, and it like to have frozen my face. I made it into the barn, and I'm not sure who was the happiest, me or the horse.

The next morning, I went to the pasture and fixed the fence where the steers broke the wires down. I was not worried about them getting out again that night because cattle won't go against the wind blowing that hard. And the broken fence was two hundred yards north of the corner where the cattle stayed the rest of the night.

All was well, except I caught the flu, and our water pipes in the house froze up, and poor old dad had to spend the next day under the house pretending he was a Plumber. I couldn't help because I had a fever of 102 and was sicker than a dog. I think I stayed home from school the whole week, but finally got better and, despite the loss of some weight, none the worse for wear.

Being off from school with the flu also helped my foot heal a little more so I could play basketball. I wasn't going to miss playing for a little thing like a broken foot anyway.

The senior class decided that we needed to have a Christmas party. Jack and Carolyn were by now, in December, always together. Angie Baby, the teacher, had a boyfriend as well, so I invited a girl I had gone with on and off for three years. The party included having dinner in Amarillo and then going to a show. In 1961, Morse had neither a restaurant nor a movie house.

Diann Hanner, the girl I was taking, lived in Borger. I told the group I would drive to Borger and get her, and we would meet up at the Williams grocery store on the highway to Amarillo. I was still feeling the effects of having the flu two weeks ago. When we got to the Chinese restaurant in Amarillo, my stomach was a little unsettled. We got seated and the smell of the Chinese food was starting to make me sick.

To be quite honest, I had never eaten at a Chinese place, and the smell was getting to me very fast. By the time the waitress brought me my iced tea, I was not doing well at all. I made it to the parking lot and let it go. I emptied everything in my stomach in ten seconds. I had never had Chinese food, and I guess being sick with the flu and all, I couldn't handle the smell.

All was well after dinner. While everyone else ate, I sat in the car, and then we went to the show, then back to Borger on our way to Morse. Diann and I still had a good time together and started dating again in a steady sort of way.

On the morning of New Year's Eve, I got bored and went hunting for rabbits in the pasture north of the barn. I had borrowed a 22 pistol that was not a six-shooter. It was an H&R Sportsman 9-shot revolver. The pistol broke open, and you loaded the shells into the cylinder, or you could take the cylinder out of the gun. In the second option, you would load the cylinder and then put it back in the gun, close it, and shoot. We had piles of fence posts and old machinery north of the barn and there were always lots of bunny rabbits around these places. I shot all nine shells and was going to reload. I took the cylinder out and put the pistol back into the holster. I had 22 shells in my shirt pocket, so I was loading the gun while looking at a rabbit. One of the shells hung up going into the cylinder, and I hit it with my hand. I had on my senior ring that was a little big because my hands were cold. The ring had turned around, and when I hit the shell, the ring must have hit the shell because it exploded.

I dropped the cylinder and looked at my hand. My fingers were all black, and it felt like it did when I had a firecracker go off in my hand. Everything was numb, and I didn't feel any real pain except the tingling of my fingers. I shook my hand and said something like, "Wow, that was close." Then, the blood started squirting from my fingers, and I knew it was a little closer than I first thought.

I picked up the cylinder, put it into my pocket, and grabbed my hand to see where the blood was coming from. My left hand was black and bloody, and I couldn't see a thing. I started back for the house, holding my left hand with my right hand and thinking, *how am I going to tell my mother without causing a lot of panic?*

I was at the back door of the house and yelled at my mother to come to the door. I put my hand behind my back so she couldn't see all the blood. Not a good idea because when she got to the door, she could see blood dripping behind me, and she thought I had been shot in the stomach. I had to tell her very quickly that it was my left hand and I was ok.

Well, sort of ok, just a couple of holes in my fingers where the 22-long rifle hollow point went through them. Mother kind of panicked and grabbed a yellow bath towel and wrapped it around my hand. She told me to get into the car, and she would take me to the doctor's office.

This was not the best idea either. When I walked into the doctor's office, it was full of sick people and a couple of pregnant women. The pregnant gals didn't react very well to seeing a guy walk in with a yellow towel around his hand that was mostly now red with blood.

I was asked to leave and go to the emergency room at the hospital across the street and that the doctor would be there as soon as he could get there. I headed across the street and into the front door of the emergency room. The nurse got very nervous hearing I had been shot with a gun, and I didn't find out why until later when the doctor was taking the bullet out of my hand.

When Dr. Greg got to the hospital, he told me the sight of blood made two of the women sick and that I caused quite a stir. He told me if I was to get all bloody, not to come in the front door to his office ever again. I told him I was sorry for that and that from now on, I would just come to the emergency room at the hospital. We both laughed and Dr. Greg started looking at the X-rays of my hand. He started digging around on the little finger of my left hand, trying to get the bullet out. This was after he gave me a couple of shots to kill the pain. I was watching him and asked where the bullet was. The nurse thought I should not watch this but Dr. Greg told the nurse I was very experienced in this sort of thing and I was a regular customer of his. He then asked the nurse for a porcelain pan and to put it on the floor next to his feet. I thought the nurse was going to faint. She got very upset with the doctor and started telling him a patient had almost died from shock the day before after being shot in the back with a shotgun. She said the wounds were not bad and only went just under the skin, but the patient went into shock and almost died from that.

Dr. Greg told the nurse not to worry, that I was not about to go into shock, and that she should take my blood pressure if she didn't believe him. When my blood pressure was completely normal, the nurse just shook her head and said to me, "This is not affecting you at all, is it?"

"Nope," I told the nurse and that she should not worry about me at all. Getting shot, blown up, or broken up was something I was getting used to.

Dr. Greg had to cut the finger open a little more to get the large piece of bullet out from around the bone of my little finger. When he finally got the chunk of lead out, he held it in the forceps so I could see it and then dropped the bullet into the pan at his feet. When the bullet made the same sound hitting the porcelain pan as it did in the movies, the doctor just looked at me and said, "Well, we'll have you fixed up good as new again as soon as I get this thing sewed up. You'll be able to go play some football this afternoon."

Now, the nurse was getting really upset and told the doctor his actions were not something a doctor should be doing. When Dr. Greg and I just started laughing, the nurse turned and walked away. Dr. Greg said, "She just doesn't know how many times you and I have worked together."

The two cousins who were with me when I was blown up a couple of months earlier came back to our house with their parents that afternoon. It seemed like every time they came to our house, I wound up in the hospital for some reason. I took the doctor way too seriously when he said that I should go out and play football that afternoon. The four of us did play football, and I was very sorry later on that evening that we did.

We went to the show that night. The painkiller had worn off, and my hand started hurting so bad I didn't see the movie. I just sat there and moaned and moaned and moaned. I hurt like hell. The doctor had to put in three or four stitches in my finger.

The next Morse High School basketball game was not much fun for me. I had stitches in my left hand, a broken right foot, and a strained right knee. I was damned near a basket case, but I scored 22 points, had four rebounds, and played the entire game, every single minute. By the time the game was over, I could hardly move, and I was in a lot of pain. When the team went into the café to eat after the game, I told the coach I would sit in the bus and hurt.

The trip back to Morse that evening was not much fun either. In the row of seats behind me was one of our team named Gene. Gene and I didn't seem to get along very well, and I'm not really sure why he didn't like me very much. Gene was putting his feet across his seat and into me in the next seat up from him. I had asked him not to bump my knee two or three times.

And he kept making smart little remarks that he could put his feet anywhere he wanted. I poked his leg and told him to move his feet now, and before I could say anything more, his fist came from out of the dark and hit me in the cheek.

I jumped over the seat and on top of Gene and, with my good hand, hit him four or five times as hard as I could swing. The bus was stopping, and the coach was pulling me off Gene, and everyone else was yelling, and I was still hitting Gene with all the power I had left.

The next morning, when I got to school, the principal called me into his office. He wanted my side of what had happened on the bus the night before. I told him the story and he asked if I had seen Gene that morning, and I told him that I had not yet seen Gene. The principal was now giving me a very stern look and said, "Come with me." We got to the room where Gene was and looked in. It was not a pretty sight. Gene's eyes were almost swelled shut, and his lips were swelled to the point that he looked like he had been French kissed by a Mack truck. I was kind of a smart ass in those days, and I said Gene was in a car wreck last night. This was not the right thing to say to the school principal at that moment. I got suspended from school for three days for beating the hell out of a guy who desperately needed it for attitude reasons.

When I got back to school and basketball practice, I was man enough to go to Gene and tell him I was sorry that I beat the crap out of him so badly. Gene developed a new attitude after that and we got along the rest of the year just fine.

A few days later, I was sitting in typing class wondering why I was there with only one hand to type with. One of the junior class girls named Jeanie walked into the classroom and sat down beside me. She started telling me all the girls wanted to thank me for what I had done to Gene. Seems as ol' Gene was giving a lot of the girls a bad time and because I beat the holy hell out of him, he was not bothering anybody now. I told her I was glad to help. She said, "Why don't you come by tonight, and we will go get a Coke or something." I told her I would and that I'd see her that night.

Well, little did I know this was going to start something that would last a very long time. We went out that night and a lot of nights after that. I was not getting along with the girl I was going with in Borger. Well, to make it clear, we got along just fine as long as her religion didn't get into any discussions, which it did once too many times, and we had just about broken up anyway. So, I didn't think it would hurt to go out with someone else. Diann Hanner would wait for me anytime, so no problem.

Spring was here and we finally got the disastrous basketball season over with. It was track time, and I thought I stood a chance of winning a district medal. I could run 100 yards in a football suit in 9.9 seconds. I was fairly good at 440 yards and the 220. So, when the district track meet came about, I thought I could win something.

The day of the track meet the weather was cloudy and drizzling some, and very cool. The 100-yard dash I entered was coming up, and I thought I was ready. The cool weather and the fact that I didn't warm up very much turned out to be a disaster,

I pulled a hamstring and didn't finish. The coach came over to me after the race. He told me I was the school's only hope to win a medal, and now I wasn't going to be able to run the long races.

I told him, "You're right. I can't run, but enter me in the pole vault, and I will win a district medal in that." The coach said to me, "Have you ever tried the pole vault?

"Sure," I told him, "I had Jack show me how yesterday, and I cleared two feet higher than our pole vaulter has ever jumped."

He looked at me and said, "Are you sure," I just winked at the coach and said, "Enter me, and I'll show you." Coach Hensley had seen me do some pretty wild things that year, and he believed me enough to enter me.

Our pole vaulter had the flu and didn't even come to the meet, so I had to borrow a pole from another school. It was an aluminum pole that didn't bend, but that was alright with me because ours didn't either. I did enough to win third place in the district in the pole vault and I never tried it again.

The rest of the spring of 1962 went by fast and furious, and it turned warm, and May was here. I was going to graduate from high school. I asked Dr. Winfred Moore to speak at the Baccalaureate service, and he accepted. Dr. Moore was one of the leading Baptist preachers and soon to be the head of Wayland Baptist University. I had good contacts in those days and it made me look good to my peers. Dr. Moore had been the pastor of the First Baptist Church in Borger when I was a little kid, and I'd known him for ten years or more.

After the graduation ceremony on May tenth, the senior class left for Rockaway Beach, Missouri, for our senior trip. There were three seniors and two sponsors. The sponsors were the school superintendent and his wife, who treated this trip as a second honeymoon. Miss Ferguson, the senior class sponsor, quit at the end of the school year and left town, never to be seen in Morse again. The other two seniors were Jack Gibblin and Carolyn George. They had gotten engaged a month before school was out and got married at the end of summer. I know it seems very young in the 21st century, but don't you see this was 1962? Jack had his life in order; at least, he thought it was in order. They, the Gibblin family, were big farmers, and Jack didn't hurt for money. So, the senior trip was two couples in love and little ol' me. Just as I wanted it, me, myself, and I, this was going to be great.

We got to Rockaway Beach about noon the following day and got unpacked. I went out to explore the sunny beaches and the sunny beach babes. About six that evening Stinnett High School pulled in and was staying in the lodge next to the ones we were in. I started talking to a big group of the Grads from Stinnett that evening, and when they had their class meeting around a big bond fire that night, they elected me an honorary class member from Stinnett. This was really good because they had about thirty-five class members and this was a good group to run around with.

We had made a lot of money that year for the senior class trip, selling food at basketball games and the Halloween carnival. We had thirty-eight dollars to spend each day. In 1962, that was a lot of money to just have fun with per week, let alone per day. I was rich and acted like it that week. I rented a ski boat one day, and four of us went skiing on the lake. The boat cost twelve dollars per hour. I rented it for two hours, and we had a great time. Girls from everywhere were watching us because we had a big ski boat, and this was great.

⟡Chapter Five⟡

We got back to the Texas panhandle at the end of a fun week, and the real world started. No more school, at least for the summer, and the rest of our lives started to become a reality. I needed to find a job that paid more than thirty-five dollars per week. That meant I had to look outside of my dad's farm for such employment. I worked at the lumberyard for a while. Then on a farm in Oklahoma until the farmer wanted me to pump up a flat tire on the rear of a tractor with a bicycle pump.

The farmer was one of the most unforgettable characters I've met in my life. His name was Ole Knutson, and he was the brother of Emil Knutson, who farmed in the Oklahoma panhandle in the early 1900s. Emil was a very big farmer that almost everyone knew about. Ole was not a big farmer but farmed over a thousand acres. Ole was not living in modern times; he stayed the same as if it were just after WWI. He lived in a two-room house that was attached to the barn. There was no electricity, no running water, and no bathroom in the house. I managed to stay and work for him for almost two weeks. And when Ole wanted me to pump the massive rear tractor tire up with a small bicycle pump, I quit at the end of that day. He wondered how I pumped the tire up so fast, and I was not about to tell him I used propane in the tire. The propane got the job done in about thirty seconds. It would have taken me all day to pump the tire up with the little bicycle hand pump.

Ole had some other problems he told me about that made him a little weird. These stemmed from his experiences in WWI. Seems as though he was a horseback messenger, and when the horse got shot out from under him, he played dead so the German soldiers would not know he was still alive and shoot him. He said he had to lie next to the dead horse for three days and never move. I thought about how that might have been done and it almost made me sick at the thought.

I decided it was time to go back to Spearman and find a job. Living in a barn with no electricity, running water, or much of anything else was not exactly what I wanted at the time. That summer, I did a lot of jobs like plowing, working construction, and pumping gas at what was known in 1962 as a filling station. Later, it would be known as a service station that offered no services except to take your money for very high-priced gasoline.

In September of 1962, I started college at Panhandle State University in Goodwell, Oklahoma. My roommate in the dorm was a friend from Spearman by the name of Ardell Black. We got all settled in and started classes, and I realized very quickly that I didn't like it there. I didn't like the classes I was in, I didn't like the dorm, and I didn't like the school period. I went through the motions for a couple of months trying to get adjusted, but the longer I was there, the more I didn't like the place. Ardell didn't care for it much, either. One night, we got talking about how badly we didn't like the place and decided to join the Navy.

The next day, we went to Amarillo and did just that, joined the Navy. After taking all the tests and having our butts looked at in the physical examination, they told us we had three days to think about it. If we still wanted to be in the Navy, send in the card we were given, and we would be sent a time to be inducted into the service. I never sent mine in and stayed home, but Ardell wound up in the Navy for four years.

I worked at a little bit of everything that year. I farmed, did construction, and worked at a lumberyard until my dad bought a filling station in Spearman. I ran that most of the time for the big sum of three hundred dollars a month.

I married Jeanie Womble on July 12, 1963. The war in Southeast Asia was just getting started, and being married helped me stay out of it. That was not the reason I got married; it was just one of the fringe benefits. Jeanie and I moved into a little apartment in Spearman, and things in our lives went pretty smoothly until January 1964.

The service station did some credit business in the form of selling gas to farmers and others on credit and hoping to get paid at the end of each month. My dad was a great guy with a very big heart and this caused us some problems with the credit business. We had five or six customers that wouldn't pay. They didn't want to be cut off from buying gas; they still wanted that, but paying the bill at the end of the month was what they didn't like to do.

I had to do most of the collection work for this company, and I used every little clever way I could think of short of using a gun to collect the money owed us.

One customer came in one day to fill his tank, and I noticed he had a Colt 45 army pistol lying in the seat of his car. I started talking to the guy about shooting and how much I liked hunting. I told him I had never shot a Colt 45 automatic. Being somewhat of a nice guy, he said, "Take my Colt 45 and go shoot it. You will like it." I did just that, and I must admit I had fun shooting his pistol. About a week later, he came into the station, filled up his car, and then said, "How did you like shooting the 45?" I told him I really liked the gun. In fact, I told him, "I liked it so much I think I will keep it until you pay your gasoline bill." He got very mad, but I had the gun and didn't give it back. He didn't pay his bill, so I sold the gun and made fifty bucks to boot.

One day in January, a customer came in. He was very drunk and said he didn't like getting a letter from us telling him we could not give him any more gasoline until he paid the three months' worth of bills he owed us. "I need this gasoline now," he said, and I had to tell him that we were sorry but he had to pay us now before we would give him any more gas. He got very mad and left, but for some reason, I knew he would be back. About an hour later, he was back, but with his son, who was bigger than he was. The son stood six feet three and weighed about 250 pounds. At five-eight and 170, I was not going to be a willing participant in a knockdown drag-out fight with these two men.

I knew the older man had a very bad temper and had a habit of doing some very stupid things. As I will explain I knew these guys very well. I told the son I didn't want any problem with them. I told him your dad was very drunk and he should take his dad home and come back to discuss the bill when he was sober. The dad didn't like me talking to the son and not to him and started pushing me in the chest with his hands and cussing like a sailor. I told him to stop and get out and go home now. He didn't like that either and took a knife out of his pocket and pointed it at me.

That was the wrong thing to do. There was a short tire iron lying on the desk in the station. I hit the older man in the shoulder and neck with it. He went down like a sack of potatoes, and the younger one came at me very fast. I hit him in the face with a quart of Quaker State Oil, 30 weight. It was enough weight because he went to the floor in a heap as well. One had blood coming from his neck the other had blood coming from his nose and mouth. I can't remember who the two guys were that came in about that time, but I was very glad to see anybody about then. Oh, in 1964 the cans of oil were made of tin, not paper like they are today. So, hitting someone in the face with a quart of oil in 1964 was not fun for the hittee at all. The two guys called my dad, and when he got there, the whole thing was over, and my dad's brother and his son had gone home to lick their wounds. This was the man I was named after, who was also my dad's twin brother. His son, my cousin, was the one that I had just kicked the crap out of.

My uncle was not much of a man in my book because many times in his life, my dad bailed him out of just about every kind of problem imaginable, and this was the kind of thanks he got. Not paying for his gas and then wanting to fight when asked for the money.

Well, I had enough of this and just about everything else in Spearman, Texas so I moved to Oklahoma City and got a job with BF Goodrich tires delivering tires, batteries, and accessories. It was not bad, and I became like a cab driver, knowing just about every street in town. I worked there for about seven months when I started noticing some very strange things going on in the office. I have always had a knack for seeing what no one else could see, especially when something was going wrong. It seemed someone in the outfit was taking money and items from the warehouse and doing everything possible to hide the evidence. I took off a Friday in September to go to Texas for the weekend, and when I got back the poo-poo had hit the fan. I guess someone in the company was watching all this, and when I was not there, they were caught in the act. I talked with them about it all and found out they thought I was the one doing the stealing until it happened while I was gone in to Texas. The culprit was found out and fired and the manager and I had a long talk about all that had happened. It made me very mad that I was the one suspected of this. They said they were sorry for thinking I was the one stealing from the company and hoped I was not too mad. I told them I wasn't and that all was fine. It was not fine. I was mad as hell, but I didn't say a thing.

71

While I was in Texas I visited with an uncle in Pampa, Texas, who was working on a job at a chemical plant. The company was building in a lot more areas. My uncle told me I could get a job there as his helper in the pipe fitting area. It paid a lot more than I was making in Oklahoma City. With all that had been going on with BF Goodrich, I decided to move to Pampa and take the job with Fish Engineering.

We moved back to Texas, and I started working as a pipe fitter's helper at the plant in Pampa. A cousin named Gary Boozer also worked there, we did a lot of hunting, and visiting during the months we lived there.

One Friday in December 1964 or January 1965, as we were getting off work and clocking out, there was a list of names on the bulletin board. My name was on the list. This list contained the names of those laid off as of then. Well, I was in Pampa with no job and not much money to stay there if I couldn't find work very fast. About 100 guys were laid off at the same time, and all were looking for a job so finding something was not looking very good.

After a couple of weeks of looking and finding nothing I was in Spearman and found a job in one afternoon. And so we moved back to the old hometown, so to speak.

A friend of mine named Little Joe Hendrix and I went to work for a company that laid pipelines for oil rigs to supply water to the rig. A case tractor had been modified with a set of tongs that screwed two-inch pipe together. The pipe was in thirty-foot lengths and we would put in about two miles of the pipe for the oil rigs to get water. Oil rigs used a lot of water for drilling the oil wells. They would set up the rigs, and it would take about three or four weeks to drill the well. Then, we would move the pipe to the next well that was to be drilled. We had about fifteen of these rigs running so we were very busy putting in or taking out the pipelines for the water.

This was the dirtiest job I've ever had. Little Joe and I would pick up a piece of pipe, stick it into the tongs and then hold the pipe while the tongs screwed it together. Each piece of pipe weighed about seventy-five pounds, and if a little bent, it was darn hard to hold the pipe while the machine screwed it together. The pipe was also very nasty so we got so dirty we would need to take two baths to get clean every night. In the early '60s, most houses only had tubs and not showers as they do today. The water in the tub and the tub got very dirty if you had an abundance of it on your person.

The guy who ran the pipe-laying company caught the flu and finally got so sick he couldn't come to work. I told him I could run the tractor and get the job we're on finished in time for the oil rig to start drilling. He had never had anyone work for him that could run the thing, but I did it, and we laid over two miles of pipe in a very rough area near Canadian, Texas.

To get the pipe to the rig, Bennett had a Dodge Truck and flatbed trailer. Joe and I loaded the two miles of two-inch pipe on the trailer, and I drove the truck to Canadian, Texas, to lay the pipe. The land in the panhandle of Texas is mostly flat, but around Canadian, it becomes very hilly going into the river bottom.

I was gunning along about sixty miles an hour going up and down the hills so overloaded that if caught the fine for the weight would have been more than I could have ever paid. I looked to the top of the next hill and saw a little girl holding a big dog standing in the middle of the road. I started breaking as fast as I could, and the little girl didn't move. I got the truck to the right as far as I could without getting off the pavement. As heavy as this thing was, it would go over in a New York second if I got off into the soft dirt at the edge of the road. The way this truck was built, it was very hard to see next to the front wheels and I was now starting to slide a little bit from the hard breaking to get this monster shut down. I felt the truck hit something and go under the tires, both front and rear duels.

The truck stopped, and I got out to see the little girl still standing, but the dog was dead. The mother of the little girl ran into the road where we were standing and started yelling at me. "You killed my hunting dog." I got very mad and stuck my finger in the woman's face and started yelling back at her. I told her off and how stupid she was for letting the little girl stand in the middle of a road holding a dog while the big fat woman just stood on the side of the road looking. I told her I only missed the kid by inches and she should be very glad the dog was dead and not her daughter. I told her maybe she should have had enough brains to get the dog to the other side of the road when a truck going sixty miles an hour was coming at them.

Then, the shock of my words hit home. She could see I was telling her the truth—she almost lost her kid and the dog. She calmed down, grabbed the little girl in a big hug, and told me she was very sorry for what she had just said. I told her I was very sorry about the dog, and I helped get what was left of the dog out of the road.

When I finally got the pipe to the location, I had calmed down also. We laid the pipe in the rain and got back to Spearman about nine that evening.

Little Joe and I worked for Bennett longer than anyone ever because the work was so hard and dirty. Bennett had no application for this type of job and ragged on us all the time. We worked in the rain, snow, blowing sand, and just about every bit of the worst possible areas in the Panhandle. Joe and I started looking for other work and I found out a new pipe plant was being built in Spearman. I applied there and got a job. Little Joe went back to being a cowboy on a ranch around Miami Texas.

Bennett was very sorry we quit when he couldn't find anyone who could work like we did. People don't know what they have until they lose it. I think a lot about things like that and started developing my own philosophy on life in general, which is not Plato, but I thought it was ok.

The pipe plant made concrete pipe about twenty-four inches in diameter, and each piece was about eight feet long. These were poured into molds and stacked in rows in the plant until the next day. Each pipe was then stacked outside in large areas until trucks took it to wherever it was to be used.

The second day I worked there, the plant foreman asked me if I knew how to operate a forklift. I could drive anything, I thought so I said, "Sure I can." When I did, and very well, I might add, they wanted me to teach some of the other workers how to run the three types of forklifts they used each day. I became the instructor, and this gained me some respect from the foreman. I think he knew I really didn't have any experience, but I did one hell of a job teaching a bunch of guys something I had only watched a few times.

A week or so later, the foreman asked me if I could weld and I said sure I could, so I became the guy that fixed whatever broke in the plant. I had fooled them again because I wasn't very good at welding, but I became good enough before they figured anything like that out.

One of my few talents was I could see something and then do it myself, very easily. I learned just about everything the pipe plant did and how to do it myself. I was asked to learn how to operate the pipe-making machinery. That is the pipe plant itself. This I had to learn with the help of the man who did it every day. I learned very quickly and was making pipe by the second day. They were very glad because the plant operator, in the beginning, didn't have a backup if he had to take off for any reason.

About this time in the spring of 1965, Shamrock Oil and Gas Company started hiring people because of a strike at its gasoline plant in Dumas, Texas.

I was shooting trap every weekend and was doing very well when the largest Shamrock dealer in the Panhandle asked me to shoot for them. Kind of a sponsorship in that they paid for all my entry fees in turn for me wearing their shirt at the trap shoots. I got to keep all that I won also.

When Shamrock started hiring people the dealer told me to go and apply for a job with them. When he told me what they paid, I didn't let my shirttail hit my butt before I was in Dumas filling out an application.

Now, in the fall of 1964, there was a company in Spearman that sold farm equipment and decided to put in a Chrysler Plymouth dealership with the farm equipment. Can't do that in the big cities, but this was not the big city. It was a little farm town in the Texas Panhandle, and they could do this in 1964. I went there for their opening along with just about everyone else in town. Plymouth was coming out with a new car called the Barracuda, and I really liked the way the car looked in the pictures. So, I got to talking with the owner of the dealership about buying one. I had a 58 Chevrolet and we traded with the dealer ordering me a new Barracuda Competition Coupe. It was called a Formula S and I didn't know at the time that only 500 of these were to be made. Anyway, I got one of these little monsters. It had a 273-inch engine, four speeds on the floor, and not much else.

Well back to the filling out of the application for Shamrock Oil and Gas. As I said, Shamrock was having a strike, and they had pickets at the front gate as I drove into the plant where Shamrock's offices were located. No problem going in, but getting back out was another thing. They, the guys on the picket line, asked me why I went into the plant. I was stupid enough to tell them that I went in there to fill out an application to go to work for Shamrock. I guess a union strike was something left out of my education in the Texas Panhandle. Hell, I was just a good ol' country boy who was half-ass smart but not much skilled in street smarts. I got a good lesson in diplomacy on the way out. They wanted to whip my ass for going in there to fill out an application. I was driving the bad-to-the-bone Plymouth Barracuda. If they wanted to whip my ass, they were going to have to catch me first. That was going to be very hard to do, I thought as I said something like, "You guys go take a flying bite of a wild cat's ass."

Three or four of the guys jumped into a '62 Impala SS, and the race was on. In two miles, they didn't know if I was headed to Canada or Old Mexico. I was out of sight and gone at over 120 miles per hour. The little Chevy couldn't keep up with the Barracuda even in third gear, let alone fourth gear.

About a week later, I got a call from the manager of the pipeline division at Shamrock asking me if I wanted to go work for them at Clawson Station. Sure, I told them, and when do I start? They wanted me there in a week, and I said I would be there.

I had to go to Dumas to take a physical, fill out all the paperwork, and go to their orientation for a couple of hours. I will be ready to start the next Monday.

✒Chapter Six✒

I went to work for Shamrock Oil and Gas Company at their pump station known as Clawson Station. It was five miles west of Gruver, Texas, on the Stratford Hwy. This pump station consisted of three big oil tanks; two were 50,000 barrels each, and one 20,000 barrels. The pump house had seven electric motor pumps that could pump about 10,000 barrels of oil per day. There was a garage that would hold about six cars and a little firehouse with the cutest little fire truck you ever saw. They told me it was for insurance only and that if the place ever caught on fire to get the hell out of there as fast as I could.

The refinery at Dumas had a fire a few years earlier, and five men were killed by the explosions in the oil tanks. I remembered the fire and said, "If this place catches fire, I will haul ass very quickly."

I had been there about a month when the district manager came in one morning and wanted to look around. We kept the place spotless. The pumps were wiped down daily, and the painted red floors were polished and waxed. At the corner of the pump house was a little room where we had test equipment. There was a crack in the floor with some white paint which must have been spilled some time before I was there. When James Gobin saw the crack with the white paint in it, he said, not asked, "Must be bird shit in the crack."

"No sir, I told him, it's paint, and I will get it out of there when I can." I think I pissed him off by not agreeing with him, and he never forgot it. I didn't realize then that I had made an enemy of the District Manager.

Things went pretty smoothly the first year at Clawson Station. I kept the books, mowed the lawn, painted the pumps, polished the floors, and watched the world go by most of the time. I would work about one day a week and the rest of the time piddled around to pass the time. It was a good job but boring most of the time by myself.

I think with the farm work and oil company job I learned to entertain myself rather well. I always had a big imagination, and I could pass the time thinking about just about anything.

I built a car in the garage that had a 16-horsepower engine and a four-speed gearbox with the help of the manager. It would only go about twenty miles per hour in high gear, but in first or second gear, it would pull a house down. We had a four-foot grass mower, which was self-propelled, but most of its power was used to move the mower, not mow the grass. I disconnected the power to the wheels, built a hitch to hook it up to the little tractor (car) we had built, and now, with all the power going to the blades of the mower while it was being pulled by the tractor, it would mow like crazy. Clawson Station was sitting on two and one-half acres, so mowing the place did take a lot of time before my little invention.

Everything went along smoothly that year at work and at home. We lived in Spearman, and I drove the nineteen miles each way to work and back. We had a little house rented in Spearman which was across the street from the funeral home, next door from two old guys that were very strange. One of the guys was a direct descendant of the Queen of England. His name was Otto Dockins, and his sister was Cassie Schrivers. Both were royal families of England.

Otto and the guy who lived with him were plumbers and ran a small plumbing business out of their house. They had a big red dog; I'm not sure what kind of dog it was, but a big one with long hair. One day I was taking out the trash to the alley

79

when this dog ran up behind me and barked. I turned to see the strangest haircut they could have given a dog. It had been shaved over its entire body except around the head and neck. The damned thing looked like an African Lion. The surprise was more than the paper sack I was carrying could stand. After laughing myself silly it took me fifteen minutes to pick up all the trash and put it into the trash barrel.

My brother Ronny had quit college in the fall of 1965 and joined the Navy. He went to boot camp in San Diego, California, at a place called Coronado Island. When Christmas time came around, he was to get out of boot camp. With the holidays and all the Navy people leaving San Diego, he could not get a flight home. Not even a bus ticket was possible until after Christmas. My dad called me on the evening of December 21st and asked if I was off for the next four days. I told him I was and asked what he needed me to do. He told me of the phone call from Ronny saying they would get out on the 23rd but could not get home for a week because of the holidays. My dad was not one to sit and think about what to do. He told Ronny we would come and pick them up. It was only 1,300 miles to San Diego, but to my dad, this would not be a problem. I asked my dad when he wanted to leave, and he said he would come pick me up in twenty minutes. My dad was not much for wasting time when there was something to do.

I jumped in the tub and was ready when he picked me up thirty minutes later, and we headed for California. I loved adventure, and since I had not been to California since I was a baby, this was going to be quite an adventure. I drove while Dad slept, and he drove while I tried to sleep. The next afternoon, we were at the navy base on Coronado Island, California finding out from Ronny they would not get the fourteen-day leave until the 24th. This did not faze my dad; he accepted what the military did because I think after three years in the army in WWII, he knew how the military did things.

We got back to the car after a boat ride across the San Diego Bay and headed to Los Angeles. My dad had some cousins there he had not seen in thirty years. My dad already had their addresses and phone numbers with him, so it would give him a chance to visit them again after all these years. He also had an aunt that lived in Long Beach who we went to see while we were there.

We got to Los Angeles and got a room just south of Knott's Berry Farm, and my dad called his cousin who lived in the area. We saw them for a little while, then went to Knott's Berry Farm that evening.

The next morning, we went to see my dad's aunt from Long Beach, and they wanted to take us to Hollywood. The cousin we saw the night before had a daughter we hadn't seen, and she wanted to go with us to Hollywood, so we picked her up and headed for Los Angeles.

I had on a cowboy hat, jeans, and boots, and when we got out of the car next to Grauman's Chinese Theater, I was going to leave the hat in the car. My dad's aunt and the cousin said to leave it on because you really look like a real cowboy. I wasn't sure what they meant, but I did as I was told and walked to the front of the theater to see all the stars' footprints on the sidewalk. I had no idea what I was getting into. People started asking me for my autograph and telling me how much they liked the last movie I was in and that they loved the TV show. This cousin of ours was nineteen and really a very good-looking girl, and she stayed right next to me all the time we were there. I wasn't sure but as I think back on it, she fit the part of the model that would be with such a big movie star like they thought I was.

I just smiled and signed their books, and thanked them for liking my movies. I signed over thirty autographs while we were there, and Linda, the cousin, was having a blast with all the attention she was getting.

I think I was a little naive about all that was going on because I didn't know that just about everyone in Los Angeles wanted to be in the movies and the look we had fit the part just right. We looked around Hollywood for a while then headed back to Long Beach to my dad's aunt's house to have dinner.

I knew I was from the backwoods when the ladies wanted food from a new place called Taco Bell. I told them I never heard of this restaurant, but it sounded good to me and my dad.

The cousin and I were chosen to go get the food from Taco Bell. Linda sat as close to me in the car as she could, and we drove to get the food. That afternoon late, actually at sundown, when we were back at her house, I said I had never seen the Pacific Ocean and asked how far it was to the beach. Linda said it was only a mile from their house, and she would show me the Ocean. We got into my dad's car, drove to Huntington Beach, and walked out onto the beach. Wow, what a sight for a country boy from Oklahoma. The ocean was quite a sight. As we were walking along the beach, Linda was starting to act like I was her long-lost kissing cousin. I asked her about the beach party movies and what it was really like surfing, singing, and all the stuff in the movies. Linda said, "Well, not really like in the movies. The kids mostly come to the beach at night to drink beer and screw."

I took her back to her house, and the next day, which was Christmas Eve, we drove back to San Diego to pick up Ronny and Don Archer. We drove all night to get back to Texas but we were there in time for Christmas.

Ronny had sixteen days leave before he, Don Archer, and Roddy Woodson were headed for New Jersey, where they would be stationed for training in the Navy. I went back to work at Clawson Station the day after I got back from California and things got back to a normal routine again.

The spring of 1966 started off just fine with the weather in the Texas Panhandle. Spring storms, wind, and cold one day warm the next.

Ronny started parachute jumping in January and really loved it and I guess he was very good at it. When he would call that's about all he would talk about. The Navy thought he must have been very good because they put him on their jump team by the end of February. They named him the Pinecone Kid because it seemed he had a habit of landing in the trees. The parachute equipment in 1966 was not what it is today, where they can be guided by pulling cords and changing direction very easily.

Ronny would call me and tell me about making ten or more jumps each week and how much fun it was. He was doing well at hitting a very small target from 10,000 feet up. I would laugh and ask, "Why would anyone want to jump out of a perfectly good airplane?" He kept telling me how much fun he was having and that he really loved parachute jumping. He would say when he got another two weeks' leave, he would come home and show me how to jump from an airplane with a parachute on. I kept saying well, I'll think about it maybe.

On Saturday, May 7 I was sitting in the little office at Clawson Station having a sandwich for lunch when my wife and one of my mother and dad's neighbors came into the office. Jeanie didn't say hello, and she just blurted out Ronny was killed in a plane crash that morning at a parachute jumping contest in Pottstown, Pennsylvania.

This was a shock, to say the least. I just sat there for a minute, waiting for what Jeanie had just said to sink in. Jeanie had tears in her eyes, the same with the neighbor lady and I didn't really know what to say to them. I asked where my mother and dad were. Jeanie said they were at their house, and I asked them to take me there. I thought about all the things Ronny and I had done in our lives that were dangerous, but we always came out just fine.

We got back to Spearman and went through all the things one goes through when something like this happens. The funeral was the next Friday, and the whole town, plus hundreds of others, were there. It was one of the largest crowds at something like this in Spearman's history. Ronny was one of the most popular kids the town had ever seen. There were girls there from everywhere and some from foreign countries. Ronny got around with the girls, and I guess from everywhere. It was the saddest event I have ever attended, still to this day, maybe not strictly for me but for all who were there. I think the saddest day for me was my dad's death. That was sixteen years ago, and I still miss him a lot. Ronny's death was a great loss for all of us. He will be missed by the many who knew him and loved him as I did. Life goes on, and I will go on with all my memories of him and all the things we did in his short life. Ronny would have been twenty-one in August of the year he died if he had lived another four months.

I went back to work and hoped all would be okay with my folks. As time went on, the next month, their spirits were lifted with the birth of my oldest son, Roger Thomas West. Roger was born on June twenty-fifth, and I think that helped Ma and Pa get over the death of Ronny a little. I was a dad myself now, and I started thinking about all the good times we would have together. This also helped me in getting over the loss of my only brother.

We, Jeanie and I, had moved to Gruver so we would be closer to my job. Now, I only had to go five miles to work each way instead of the eighteen miles from Spearman. I liked Gruver even though it was smaller than Spearman with nothing to do unless you had the imagination I possessed.

I got acquainted with a guy named Roy Red. Roy and his wife Eileen had twin girls who were within a month of Rogers's age. We all got to be good friends and did a lot of hunting and fishing together. We cut down an old Cadillac to make a rabbit-hunting buggy.

One evening, while working on the buggy Roy saw what he thought was a snake go under a piece of tin roofing that was close to where we were. I had on welding gloves, so I told Roy to get a shovel, and I would lift the piece of tin up. When I did, the snake struck and hung his fangs in the seam of the glove right beside my thumb. It took me only about a half second to come out of the glove, and Roy hit the snake just behind the head. It was a diamondback Rattlesnake about five feet long. That was a little bit close, but once again, no harm to me. We went right back to working on the hunting buggy. The darn thing weighed in at 2,800 pounds, even after we cut the body off the car. They don't make them like that nowadays; this car was all there and very heavy. We installed aircraft landing lights and a spotlight, and we had the perfect rabbit-hunting buggy. The thing started out as a 1954 Cadillac Fleetwood that must have weighed 6,000 pounds because every part of the car was very heavy. We started hunting rabbits for a mink farm in Stinnett, Texas, for twenty-five cents per rabbit. Heck, it was fun and profitable; we would shoot about seventy-five rabbits per night. We did this a couple of nights each week during the summer of 1966.

One weekend in late September, we decided to go to Fredrick, Oklahoma, to see my cousins there. My cousin Jimmy was at college, so Gary Boozer and I spent the weekend doing fun stuff, sort of.

That Saturday morning, we decided to go hunting and shooting in the sandhills north of Tipton, Oklahoma. We hadn't seen much to shoot at and we were driving south down this very sandy road when Gary saw a man in the bar ditch lying down.

We got to the top of the hill about a hundred yards from the guy, stopped the car, and got out. When we walked to the back of the car, the man who was lying in the ditch got up and was standing in the road. He had on a light blue sweater and he had his right hand in the sweater pocket. He had blood all over the side of his face and didn't look to be in too good condition. He was staggering somewhat and mumbling. When he saw us standing there looking at him, he started yelling. "I'm going to kill you white boys," as he pulled a very large hunting knife from the sweater pocket.

We were out here to do some shooting and hunting, so we were very well-armed. We had a WWI 30-06, 45 automatic, two 22 caliber rifles, and two 12-gauge shotguns. We were getting a little nervous about this guy, but we weren't afraid of him. We asked him how he got out here and how badly he was hurt. He started saying things like the others left me for dead and that they were trying to kill him. The man was black, and from what we could see, he was hurt, but we didn't know how badly.

There was a house about a mile down this road Gary said, and we jumped back into our car and headed for the house. We asked the woman there if she had a phone so we could call the sheriff. She got the sheriff on the phone and handed me the receiver. The deputy asked for a description of the guy and said he looked like one of the men who robbed a store and shot one person in Altus, Oklahoma, that morning. He got the sheriff on the phone, and the sheriff asked who we were. When we told him, he wanted to know if we had guns with us. We told him what we had with us, and he then said, "Do you guys think you can stop this guy from getting away?"

"Hell yeah," we told him that we could stop just about anything with what we were carrying in the car. The sheriff told us there were four of them, and they might come back that way.

We told him we could handle it and asked, "How do you want us to stop this guy?"

The sheriff said, "Shoot the SOB if you have to, but don't let him get away. I will deputize you when I get there." We were on our way.

Gary and I thanked the woman and headed back up the road to where we left this dude. We talked about what we were going to do when we found him. I asked Gary if he could shoot him if we had to. I knew we both could if it came down to it. When we got there, the guy was not on the road, and we got out and started looking around. I had the 30-06, Gary had a 12 gauge, and I also had the 45 in my belt.

There were a lot of trees to the east about a hundred yards away, and Gary said, "I think I see him in those trees." We walked toward him about thirty yards when he came out from behind a tree, holding the knife and yelling at us. I aimed the 30-06 at the tree just to his left and pulled the trigger. Bark flew from the tree and the guy jumped behind another tree on his right. This tree was very large, and I took aim again at the middle of the trunk and fired. This time, when he came out from behind the tree, he had his hands over his head and said, "Don't shoot me, white boys. I'm hurt bad." We told him to start walking this way and to keep his hands in the air. When he got about halfway to us, we could see he still was holding the knife. I told him, "If you don't drop the knife, I will kill you before you can take another step." He stopped and stared at me, looking very angry, and said, "You won't kill me."

"Wrong," I said as I raised the rifle to my shoulder, "You won't get another step closer; I'm warning you." I pulled the trigger. The bullet went just to the left of the guy's head, and he dropped the knife and went to his knees. He said again, "Don't shoot me, white boy. I'm hurt bad." I told him to get his ass up and start walking toward the road, and we'd get him some help.

He started walking again, and we could see the dust from a car coming very fast. Gary said very quietly, "Here is the sheriff." We were about twenty yards from the road when the sheriff and a deputy ran up and, handcuffed the guy and dragged him to their car. The sheriff thanked us and told us what they had done and how dangerous these guys were. He was very proud of us for stopping him.

Back in those days, everyone was not like they are now. No one worried about lead paint because we didn't eat that stuff. We didn't wear helmets to ride a bicycle, and we were not politically correct about everything, and yes, I would have shot the damned black guy if I had to.

About the same time, in the fall of 1966, I was promoted from running Clawson Station to a field gauger in the Farnsworth field. That area was between Spearman and Perryton, Texas. I gauged the full tanks and pumped the oil to Clawson Station.

One day in the early spring of 1966, I had pulled up to a tank battery to turn it off. As I got out of my pickup truck, I saw another car turning into the tank battery. The fella got out of the car, walked up, and asked, "Who are you?" I told him I was the pumper switcher from Shamrock Oil and Gas. Then I asked him who he was, and the man answered, "I'm Lamar Hunt Junior. I own this oil company." At that time Lamar Hunt senior was one of the wealthiest men in the United States, and his son Lamar Junior was a billionaire also. We stood there and visited for about thirty minutes, and he was very happy with the job I was doing. One of the other things that Lamar Hunt owned was the Kansas City Chiefs NFL football team.

The biggest thing about this job was the weather. In the spring and winter the weather would go from very cold to warm in one day. In the spring, this was worse because of extreme changes from cold to warm. Oil gets thicker in cold weather and thinner in the warm temperatures. The oil builds up in the pipelines when the weather changes like this. To fix the problem of some of the oil buildup, we would run a thing called a pipeline pig in the pipes. This pig would clean up the pipes so the oil could move and not stop up the pipes. As a fairly new gauger, I was not told about all I should have known about running these pipeline pigs. I had a pig in a pipeline, and it stopped. To fix the problem, I took the inlet valves out of the pump that was pumping the oil and the pig. Taking the valves increased the pressure the pump would make to about double. It moved the stuck pig, but it caused a pressure spike that was read in the field office in Dumas, Shamrock's main field office.

This was about the end of March of 1968 and the weather that year was worse than most years. It would snow one day and be short-sleeve weather two days later, then snow again. Running these pipeline pigs kept the oil moving smoothly in weather like this. I guess I didn't run enough of them that spring, and when the one I ran that day stopped, I kind of panicked. But I knew how to fix the problem if the pipeline didn't blow up from too much pressure. Taking the valves out of the pump would allow the pump to go up in pressure by four times normal. I think it went to over 200 pounds in that line to finally move the stuck pig. I fixed the problem by doing this. I will admit I was taking a chance of blowing up the pipeline with over 200 pounds of pressure, but like I said it fixed the stuck pig and didn't blow up.

My big mistake was telling the field office when they called to ask why the pressure went so high. I was honest and told them exactly what I did to fix the stuck pig and that everything was fine and running okay again. Remember when

I started with Shamrock? I might have made an enemy of James Gobin about the bird shit thing on the floor, which was really white paint? Well, I was right about making an enemy of him, and this was just the thing he was waiting for to get me back about the bird shit thing from over two years back. He called me on the radio and drove to where I was because he was at the Spearman office, which was only about fifteen minutes from me.

To make a long story short, he fired me. I think he had waited for over two years for his chance. I have always wondered what kind of person would want to have that much desire for revenge. I grew up with the idea of always being honest and not hating people the way some do. I knew man's inhumanity to man had been around for as long as there have been people on this earth, but I have never understood why.

It looks like we start over again with a career change. I wasn't really thrilled with the way Shamrock was doing things anyway. They had been bought out by a company called Black Diamond, and the new company was called Diamond Shamrock. There are always problems when some new company takes over and wants to do things a little differently.

The guy who was at Clawson Station after I was moved into the field took my place in the Farnsworth area. His name was Larry Cline, and he was a good guy.

About a month later, he was leaving the coffee shop in Spearman about five minutes to eight in the morning, just like we did each and every day when I worked there. He was about seven miles east of Spearman when an oncoming car pulling a two-wheeled trailer was meeting him. The trailer came loose from the car and the trailer hit Larry's pickup in the left front. The trailer was loaded with drill bits for drilling oil wells. The trailer was very heavy, and the car was going about seventy-five miles per hour. Larry's pickup was also going about the same speed when the trailer hit his pickup. Larry was killed instantly; it broke nearly every bone in his body. I was in Spearman that morning and heard about the wreck almost as fast as the police did. I drove out there and got to the wreck just after the ambulance had removed the body. I have seen some messes in my life, but not quite as bad as his truck (the same truck I would have been in one month earlier). The grill was pushed into the bed of the pickup, and the cab was smashed into almost nothing. No one could have survived that mess. If I had still been working for Shamrock, I would not be writing this now.

My dad and I bought three new Gleaner combines and one new truck and we went on the wheat harvest the summer of 1968. We started cutting wheat in Crowell, Texas, and finished on the North Dakota state line.

Just before the wheat was ready to cut in Crowell, my dad and I went to look at the wheat and talk to the people we had cut for in the years past. We stopped in the town of Crowell for lunch, and in the little café was a lady named Cassie Schrivers, whose brother was my next-door neighbor in Spearman. Cassie had lived in Spearman also and my dad recognized her. They started talking and Cassie was telling my dad about the hotel she owned there in Crowell. The hotel was an antique and she told my dad she had moved some of her things into the hotel for safekeeping and asked my dad if we wanted to see these things.

I have seen some pretty wild stuff in my life, but "these things," as Cassie called them, took the cake. The old hotel rooms had doors that were common for the time they were built, which was somewhere about 1900. The door she took us to was twice as thick and had a rubber seal around it. Also, there were very heavy locks on this door. When we walked into the room, my mouth dropped open. I couldn't believe what was in this room. The only piece of furniture from George Washington's home that was not in the white house in D.C. or in the Smithsonian Institute was in this room. It was a China cabinet with the cups and saucers that George and Martha drank from, and they were in this cabinet along with many other items from their kitchen.

When President Kennedy was killed in Dallas in 1963, Mrs. Kennedy had planned to go to Crowell later that day to try to buy this Cabinet from Mrs. Schrivers. But we know what happened that day in Dallas, so she did not go to Crowell to buy it.

Also in the room was a Ming Vase, a cabinet from the Ming Dynasty and many other items that were just invaluable. The contents of the room were worth about ten million dollars, and this was in 1968. As it turned out, Mrs. Cassie Schrivers was a first cousin to Queen Elizabeth of England and had acquired these things from her husband who was also of the royal family from England. How the heck all this stuff wound up in a hotel room in Crowell, Texas, I've never understood. I know that Mrs. Schrivers sort of wanted to do her own thing and didn't care much for the royal family back in the old country. Cassie Schrivers was at that time eighty-six years old, and I really can't remember when she died, but her little brother, who lived in the house next to me, left the country and was never heard from again. I guess he wound up with all that stuff and sold it somewhere.

We went out east of Crowell to Lloyd Foxx's place to look at his wheat and met up with Lloyd's son-in-law, Bill Hammonds. Now Bill was a cowboy to the bone, and we all sat down in the barn because Bill was recovering from surgery and couldn't get around real well yet. Bill started telling us about his operation, and I don't think I've ever laughed so hard in my life.

Bill had hemorrhoids, and the way he told about the operation just about killed us all from listening to the story. It had to do with getting to leave the hospital. The doctor said he had to have a bowel movement before he could go home. As I said, Bill was a real, old-fashioned cowboy, and when he got to the part of the story where he strained and strained and strained to get the job done, he said he called the nurse into the bathroom to show her that he had just crapped a fence post. The nurse helped him up from the stool, and they both looked at a turd about the size of a camel cigarette floating around in the water. We were crying we were laughing so hard. He told the nurse, "By God, go get the doctor and show him." We were now lying on our sides, crying and laughing so hard I thought I was going to die.

We started cutting Lloyd and Bill's wheat about the middle of May and moved back to Spearman to cut about three weeks later. We then moved north to Holyoke, Colorado, and cut wheat for the owner of the bank in Holyoke. We cut there for about three weeks and then moved on up to Pierre, South Dakota, where we cut oats for about two weeks.

To harvest the crops in the Dakotas, you need pickups on the combines. These are attachments that pick up the grain after it has been windrowed. The pickups get the grain and stalk off the ground and feed it into the combine. While installing these pickups, I tore a muscle in my chest, and it hurt like hell. Cutting oats is very dusty, and the oat dust was making me cough, and it was not helping my torn chest muscle at all. I went to the Doctor in Pierre, and the doctor was Chinese. His remedy was to ask me what brand of whiskey I drink and said, "I'll give you a prescription for that." The doctor, even though he was Chinese, had one hell of a sense of humor. I got Jack Daniels with his prescription and mixed it with some Coke, and I quit coughing so much.

We moved on north to Mobridge, South Dakota and cut wheat on the North Dakota state line. This was on the Sioux reservation, and most of the people we cut for were Sioux. The first wheat fields we cut were owned by Walking Elk and his wife, Chase Alone. Go figure out how she got that name if you don't have anything else to do for a couple of hours. Walking Elk told us one afternoon not to leave any gasoline in the combines overnight because the damned Indians would steal that stuff in a hurry. We didn't tell him the combines were diesel, just to see what they would do. We didn't lose any diesel after the first night and we saw three cars abandoned within a mile from his field.

I know forty years later, it would not be politically correct to mistreat our Native American brothers that way, but what the heck; we didn't tell them we were Cherokee and didn't really like the Sioux anyway. Besides, our favorite pastime while we were there was to go to the end of Main Street and watch the Indians fight on Saturday night.

We got back to the Texas Panhandle in late August and started fixing the combines to cut maize or milo in the fall. Back in those days, farmers grew a lot of maize, which was used mostly for cattle feed. There were farmers that grew corn, but not many back then. The farm crops were wheat, milo, or maize, along with cattle. There in the Panhandle, things had stayed the same as far as farming went, but now they grow mostly wheat, corn, and cotton; yes, cotton. They still raise a lot of cattle there, also. The wheat makes good pasture during the winter, and when the cattle are taken off in late March, the wheat starts to really grow with the warmer weather, and it is harvested in late June to early July.

We cut milo that fall until Christmas because the weather was very erratic. It would go from warm to snow and back to warm again. After the first of the year, I didn't have much to do to make money and decided to move to Amarillo so I could get a regular job and make a living. Roger was two years old, and Jeanie was going to have another baby in the summer.

We moved into an apartment in Amarillo along with an old friend of mine named Jimmy Stumpf. Jimmy's wife was also pregnant, and that gave my wife and Jimmy's wife something in common. I was the best man at Jim's wedding. Jim and his wife are still married today and that has been just about forty years now. Also, Jim and I are still very good friends and talk on the phone at least once a week and have done so for forty-plus years. Jim now lives just east of Charlotte, North Carolina where he has been for about twenty-five years now.

I started looking for a job after moving to Amarillo, but this was in the middle of the war in Southeast Asia, and not many jobs were to be found in the farming capital of the northern Texas Panhandle.

Jimmy was working for Glidden Paint in one of the shopping malls but was looking for something else and found a job with Met Life. He thought it would be better because the pay was based on commission selling. I met the manager of the insurance agency, and he told me I should go to work for them as well. I had not found anything else, so I decided to give the insurance business a try.

Met Life hired me, and they wanted me to go to their insurance school in Chicago for two weeks. This was going to be an experience, to say the least. I was an Oklahoma/Texas boy raised in a small town, and during the 1950s and 1960s, one could be raised fairly naïve, which would be a gross understatement. I was smart but had very little street smarts in regard to life in the big cities of this country. Life was a little bit different back then. No, it was a lot different back then in the Texas Panhandle.

I was brought up by parents who worked, both of them, and we went to church every Sunday. We ate dinner at the table every night and watched Gunsmoke, and I Love Lucy. I thought everyone in the world did the same things as we did most of the time. I later learned that must not have been true with the majority of the world. The values I learned as a kid growing up where I did were not the same as the rest of the country, let alone the rest of the world.

My dad taught us we should believe everyone was honest until they proved otherwise, that a man's word was his bond, and a handshake sealed the deal. Boy was I going to get some lessons in life outside the little area I grew up in. Sometimes, I think it has taken far too long to learn all the lessons of life. Hell, I think I am still learning them at the age of sixty-four. I'm not stupid; I'm just stubborn in some things, I guess.

I have lived in Las Vegas, Nevada now, for over seventeen years and I was forty-eight when we came here. I think I started learning street smarts at the age of forty-eight. School learning is just for getting started in life. It's like going to kindergarten before you go to school.

Anyway, I got on an airplane in Amarillo, Texas, and flew to Chicago to attend this insurance class for two weeks. We stayed in the Oxford House Hotel in downtown Chicago. Not only was this going to be a learning experience for the insurance business, but it was going to be a college degree in a big city. My first lesson was not only could you be charged more than a dime for a cup of coffee, but you needed to leave a tip that was more than the fifty cents you just paid for the coffee.

My accent was a problem as well; you see this was before the Texas accent was accepted worldwide as it is now.

96

I'm still somewhat naive about some things, ain't I? I feel I should use that word now and then so I can remember where I'm from.

Just about every time I said anything in Chicago, I had to tell them where I was from. I was asked damned near every time I said anything to anyone. Yes, I am from Texas. This did get me into some places that few others could get into being from Cleveland or someplace like that.

One evening, a few of us were walking down one of the streets in downtown Chicago and saw this bar that looked interesting, so we went in.

After a short while, I asked the bartender where the men's room was, and this was after saying, "Yes, I'm from Texas."

The bartender pointed me in the right direction of the outhouse. As I was walking to the restroom, I went past this big curtain next to what I guessed was a part of the bar where a group could meet without being seen by everyone else in the bar. Anyway, as I went past the curtain, a fellow was coming out to go to the same place I was headed and we ran into each other. Two men were following this guy, and both pulled out handguns and stuck them in my face in about half a second.

I said, "I'm sorry, sir, I didn't see you." The guy asked me, "Where are you from?" and I once again said that I was from Amarillo, Texas. The guy waved his hand at the two men with their guns drawn, and they lowered the guns and just smiled at me. The fellow I had bumped into stuck out his hand and said, "I'm Mayor Daley of the city of Chicago, and how are you doing young man."

"Very well, sir," then I had a little conversation with the mayor of Chicago.

The next day was St. Patrick's Day, and I was to find out this was a big holiday in Chicago. Where I came from, St. Patrick's Day was the day you wore a green shirt, and that was about it. In Chicago, it is a very big deal. They turn the Chicago River green and have a very big parade and lots of parties all over town. That morning at about ten, while I was on break from school, I walked across the street to the Walgreens drug store on Wabash Street in downtown Chicago. The river is across the street from the drug store and I also wanted to see what a very green river looked like.

I was walking through the drug store and started to go around the corner of an aisle when I walked into this girl headed in the other direction carrying some items she had picked up from the shelves. When we hit each other everything she was carrying wound up on the floor.

As I walked around the big city, I suppose, I was looking at everything so much I didn't always look where I was going. Well, anyway, I smacked this black lady and knocked everything she was carrying to the floor. I told her I was very sorry that I didn't see her, bent over, picked up the items, and handed them back to her. When I said I was sorry, the first thing she said back to me was the well-worn phrase, "Where are you from?"

I replied with the standard answer, "Ma'am, I'm from Amarillo, Texas and are you, Diana Ross?"

"Yes," she said, and we started talking about why I was there, how I liked Chicago, and what I was doing that evening. I asked why, and then she said she was having a party across the street at the Twin Towers and that she would like me to come to her party.

In the spring of 1969, Diana Ross was a very big star in every sense of the word. I decided to go to the party. I didn't believe I would get in after seeing how big it was and that there were two huge bodyguards at the door, not letting anyone in that didn't have a written invitation.

Bravery was one of my strong suits so I strolled right on up to the door and explained that Miss Ross was expecting me. One of the guards asked me if I was the guy from Amarillo, Texas, and I told him I was, and then he bowed and said, "Miss Ross is waiting for you at the bar." Wow, I thought as I went in and walked up to the bar. Diana Ross was standing at the bar and greeted me with a kiss on the cheek and wanted to know what I was drinking. Tom Collins, I told her, and she told the bartender I was with her and to fix me anything I wanted. She introduced me to many of her friends, and one of them was one of the Elite from, of all places, Amarillo, Texas. She was the daughter of Dick Bivins, who the big football stadium in Amarillo is named after. She was a true jet setter and the first one I had ever met. She wanted to know all about me, where I lived and what I did, and did I want to go back to her hotel room and screw. I have seen forward, but not like this, and I was not ready. I didn't know what to do or say at this point. She was about five or six years older than I was and very good-looking. The thing was, I had never run into someone that forward, and I wasn't sure I could have handled the situation any worse. I think I just stood there with my mouth open and said something like, "What?"

I was married, and I was not going to get into bed with someone that every newspaper in the area would know about since they followed every move she made. I could see the headlines in the gossip columns of the Amarillo paper that I had screwed Dick Bivin's daughter while in Chicago. See, I told you I was naive. Anyway, I found a way out of that with the help of Diana Ross, who I think knew what Miss Bivins was doing to this poor little country boy from the sticks. I'm not sure that Diana Ross saved me from her just for the sake of being nice but being selfish. I wasn't going to find out either way. So, I thanked her for her kindness and for inviting me and told her it was a very nice party. But the next day, I had to go to the insurance school, and I should be going.

I have turned down a lot of opportunities in my life, far more than most, I would bet. I was married, and that is what married people are supposed to do, isn't it? That's the way I was then, and I'm still the same guy today. Probably a little old-fashioned, but that's the way I was raised. I have never been a person who followed trendy things, either. In high school in Morse, Texas, I set the trends, and people followed me.

Anyway, I didn't screw either of those gals, and I'm glad. I had a good time at Diana Ross's party, and I left by myself.

The next evening me, and a couple of the guys were talking about going to eat in one of the fanciest restaurants in Chicago. We decided to go to the Blackhawk, which, according to the hotel people, was the best in the city. We were country boys and didn't know you needed reservations for a place like that. So, we just strolled down the street and walked right in and up to the host. As we were standing there, I looked up and saw Mayor Daley sitting in the middle of the room at a table with about six people. The Mayor also saw me at the same time and he waved and called out my name and said hello. I answered the Mayor with a, 'How you doing there, chief?'

He smiled at me and waved again. The host was watching all this, and when I said to the host, "You got a table for three Texas boys here in this place?"

The host snapped and said, "Right this way, gents." We were seated just two tables away from the Mayor and his group. I don't know who they thought we were but there were about twenty folks at the bar who were giving us very stern looks. Hell, who cares? We were eating and they were waiting for us to finish. Nice to know people in high places sometimes.

Well, I made it through the two weeks in Chicago and got to see the museums and big buildings and Diana Ross and meet the Mayor. Heck of a trip, don't you think?

I hated the insurance business in Amarillo because it was mostly weekly pay life insurance and most of my time was spent trying to get people to pay. A damned bill collector and insurance salesman, two of the most hated people in the world. I went to work selling Fords and this was the year Ford was making the crappiest car ever. The Mustang was the only car they had that was not total crap. Selling crap is tough in any market.

So, I started hauling food ~~from~~ for a big warehouse in Amarillo to supermarkets all over the northern half of Texas and New Mexico. This was not bad except for the winter weather. I think they only sent me to places where a snowstorm was expected that day.

I left Amarillo one morning at about 1:00 AM headed for Graham, Texas, and by the time I got to Vernon, Texas, the fog was so thick I had to stop because I couldn't see the end of the hood of the White Freightliner I was driving. This was worse than you might think because this was a cab over and had no hood. I finally left Vernon an hour later when I could see across the street. I got to the same store in Graham I had gone to the week before and pulled around back to unload the food. The fog and ice had collected on the power lines to the point that the lines were hanging down maybe a foot lower than normal. I hit the damned things with the corner of the trailer and ripped three of them in two. These power lines were, as I soon found out, the main lines coming from Ft. Worth. They had 30,000 volts each, and when they started bouncing around, one hit the back of the grocery store and knocked a hole in the wall big enough to crawl through. What made things worse was the hole was in the freezer of the store. One of the power lines was dancing around hitting the trailer of the truck. Now the problem was how do I get out of the truck without getting fried like a potato chip. I waited until the power line hit the trailer, then bounced across the pavement about twenty feet, and I jumped out and ran like hell to get away from the darned thing.

About that time the police and fire departments showed up with lights and sirens blaring. People were running around waving their arms and looking like they had no idea what to do. I think most of them were right about not knowing anything. I said to one of the policemen, "How about calling the power company and getting the power shut off."

"Good idea," he said and made the call.

This was no little problem; the lines were the ones that brought power to most of the town of Graham, not just the food store. Someone was going to really be pissed about this, but I didn't put the ice on the lines. I just hit the damned things. Well, to make a long story short, the total cost to fix the lines and the store cost the trucking company's insurance about $10,000.

It was the dead of winter, and the weather was not improving at all. I knew continuing to drive a truck was not what I wanted to do. One day I saw an ad in the newspaper for people to go to work for the new Bell Helicopter overhaul and modification center. It was now open at the airport in Amarillo. I went out and put in my application and was hired as a class B aircraft mechanic. I worked there until the spring of 1970. Not bad pay and it kept me off the highways in the snow. I even had carpet to stand on while putting new glass in the doors of B and G model helicopters.

In the late spring they moved me from building C to building A to work in the tail section area. I didn't like the job at all; the time passed very slowly, and some of the places they wanted rivets weren't large enough for a boy let alone someone my size. I think Bell Helicopter must have used midgets with long arms to build these things. Anyway, I decided I would apply for a job with an oil and gas company in New Mexico.

I had a cousin who worked for El Paso Gas Company in Farmington, New Mexico, for fifteen years. I had asked him if he thought I could get on with this gas company. He told me to come out there and put in my application, and he would do what he could for me.

I got into my new Oldsmobile convertible and headed for Farmington, New Mexico, the next day. It was late May, and the weather was very nice, so I put the top down on the car and drove the 500 miles to Bloomfield, New Mexico.

The next day, I went to the main office building of El Paso Gas Company. I found the personnel office and filled out the application. The next day, I headed back to Amarillo. The fellow I spoke with said it might be a few weeks, but someone would get back to me.

So, when I got home, I knew I needed to find a job again. I went back to work driving a food truck again for the same company as a year earlier.

This time, the weather was warm and hot hauling groceries to the stores. One day, a friend of mine told me about a guy who needed drivers to haul cattle to the feedlots in Colorado. It was the time of year that a lot of cattle were moved from the pastures in Texas to feedlots all over the country and many of these were in Colorado. I had been up since 1:00 AM hauling food. When I came in at about three in the afternoon, I went to the Amarillo Livestock Auction Company to find this guy who needed the drivers. He was from Texhoma, as it turned out, and I knew a lot of people there. We talked for a while about my experience, and he asked if I could take a load to Longmont, Colorado, that evening. Hell yes! I'm young and tough, and I'm ready. He said they would be ready to load about seven that evening, and I told him I would be there.

I went home to tell my wife what I would be doing and took a shower and ate then went back to the auction company to load the cattle. Seven of us left Amarillo at about nine that night, loaded with 700-pound steers for Longmont. We stopped in Lamar, Colorado, for coffee and headed up Highway 287. About two hours later, I was getting very tired and sleepy. I started the day at about four that morning and it had been a longer day than I thought it would be earlier that morning. I told one of the drivers that I might need to pull over for a while and get a nap. He told me to wait until we got to Denver, and he would help get me something to keep me going on to the feedlot.

We got to Watkins on the east side of Denver and stopped at a large Sinclair truck stop. We ordered coffee, and he asked the waitress if she had any black magic. She said she did and returned with a napkin with ten little black pills. She sat the napkin in front of me and said, "That will be five dollars, cowboy." I gave her the five bucks and took one of the little black tablets. Son-of-a-gun, I could have driven for two more days. "What in the hell is in these pills?" I asked the other driver when we got to the feedlot. He told me they were called RJS 50s, and they were diet pills. Well, that didn't sound so bad, so I kept the little pills in case I might need some help down the road sometime.

The pills were really bennies, and I'm not going to explain exactly what was in them. Anyway, the thing did the trick. We unloaded the steers and drove all the way back to Amarillo. I could have done it again without any sleep. When I got home that afternoon, I drank a glass of milk and got into a tub of nice hot water for a soaky-soak-you-clean bath. I was asleep in two minutes, and Jeanie tried for fifteen minutes to get me to wake up. I learned very fast these little pills only work if you don't eat anything or drink any milk. Not bad—you could drive 1,000 miles and get skinny at the same time. What a deal, I thought as I loaded cattle the next evening. I got to Lamar that night, and with coffee, I had another one of the little pills, and it worked like a charm. I got back to Amarillo the next afternoon and went home, took a bath, ate, loaded more cattle, and was on the road again for Colorado. Got to Lamar and more coffee and another black magic, and life was good. I got almost to Denver, and the lights from oncoming cars would stay in front of me after the car passed. Wow, this was very interesting I thought. I was tired, and the delayed action from a car passing stayed in my very tired head for a few seconds after the car passed by.

We got back to Amarillo and had the weekend off, and on Monday evening, we cranked it up again. Colorado and black magic and the money I was making. I could make more in one week of hauling cattle than I could make in a month hauling food. This was great. This went on until early August. I made two rounds to Colorado and was asked if I thought I could make one more before stopping. This was not going to be fun at all, I thought. So, being clever, I asked my brother-in-law to go with me. Bob was in college and was a farm boy, and he was looking to get married in a couple of months, so he went with me.

Bob wanted to see a resort in Colorado Springs that he and his new bride might want to go to on their honeymoon. I usually didn't go that way, but it would be four days before going out again, so why not go a little out of the way? So, I decided we could go through Colorado Springs. Sure, I told Bob, we can go that way. We will have plenty of time to look around there.

We got to Colorado Springs about one in the afternoon and looked at the resort. We even took a drive up the Cheyenne Mountain to look around there. The girl at the toll booth didn't want to let us go up there with a KW truck until I explained to her if you let these busses go up there, why not this truck? The truck had more power and more brakes, and she said, "Okay." We paid the toll and were the first big truck to go to the top of Cheyenne Mountain, I think.

The little black pill was wearing off, and I asked Bob if he thought he could drive this thing for a couple of hours while I got a nap. "Sure," he said. Now, Bob was a farm boy, as I have already said, and as such, he could drive about anything that had wheels and a steering wheel. I could, and I was sure he could. I watched him for five minutes and knew he would be fine. And told Bob to wake me when we got to the Raton Pass because it was quite a hill, and he didn't have much experience driving the big truck with the double-decker trailer. Bob was a farm boy and could drive anything, as I've already said. I woke up as we were stopping for a red light in Raton New Mexico. "Good job," I told Bob, "Let's stop and get some coffee before heading on into Amarillo."

We got back into the truck at about 2:00 AM and started down the road again. We were about twenty-five miles out of Raton, in the middle of nowhere New Mexico, with no traffic anywhere in sight, when we saw a truck stopped in the middle of the highway just sitting there with its lights on.

We stopped, and I told Bob it looked like the engine was running, and the guy behind the wheel looked to be okay. I will get out and go ask him what is wrong. I got out and hopped up on the running boards of the big Freightliner, and the driver rolled down his window. I asked him if everything was okay and he looked at me very slowly and said, "Sure is, buddy, just waiting for the train to go by."

"All right, fine, have a good one, and we'll see you down the highway."

I got back into the truck and told Bob what the guy said. Bob started laughing out loud and said there isn't any train here.

Hell, there aren't even any train tracks for thirty miles. Is he drunk? No, I don't think he's drunk. I think he has taken too many little pills called Black Magic. Sometimes known as LA turnarounds. Well, I decided I had taken all of those little pills I was going to. Crap, if they are doing that to him, I sure as heck didn't need to be doing this anymore.

I threw the rest of the black magic pills I had in my shirt pocket out the window of the truck and told myself I needed to get another job. The money was great, but the benefits sucked.

The next day, rested, I called my dad and asked if he was thinking about going hunting in New Mexico this fall. He said, "Yeah, I think I might." I asked him if he wanted to go to Farmington to look at the hunting for this fall.

Now, my dear old dad was one rare man. He was always ready to go. Anywhere, anytime, just say go and he was already in second gear headed down the road.

One day, a couple of years earlier, I was still living in Gruver and had driven over to Spearman to talk and mess around and I ran into my dad going down the street. He turned around and caught up with me, and we pulled over and he asked me what I was doing for the next couple of days. I said I wasn't doing that much and asked him what he wanted me to do. He said that Roy Bulls, his next-door neighbor, needed someone to take a load of drilling equipment to eastern Tennessee around Knoxville or someplace. "Want to go with me?" he asked.

I said, "Okay, when do you want to go."

"Right now," he told me and headed for the house. I followed him and told him I would need to go get some clothes and other stuff. He said they sell undies in most states, and we need to get going now.

Well, we got into his grain truck and went to Baker and Taylor Drilling to get the stuff they wanted hauled to Knoxville.

I had just enough time to call my wife and tell her I would see her in a couple of days because we were taking some drilling equipment to Tennessee. She had known my dad for enough years to know he did things that way, and all she could say was to have a good, safe trip.

We got the drilling equipment loaded and I found out why they would want us to do this hauling for them. It was too much for a pickup truck but not enough for them to use one of their big oil field trucks to haul. We headed for Tennessee about five that evening and got into Memphis about the time the sun was coming up the next morning. We stopped for gas and noticed a lot of army trucks were running around in the city very early that morning. We asked the guy at the service station what was going on. He said, "Didn't you hear that Martin Luther King was shot here last night?"

"No," we answered. We asked if they were expecting trouble from the blacks over the shooting.

He said, "Yes." We thanked him for the information and got the heck out of there as fast as we could. We didn't stop until we got to Nashville to have lunch.

We stayed at a motel near Knoxville and headed out to the drilling rig the next morning, very early. We found the place, and it was the strangest drilling rig I had ever seen. The thing was only about thirty feet tall, and I asked one of the workers what kind of rig it was. He said it was a raised rig. They drilled a pilot hole about four inches into a coal mine shaft and put these special bits on, and drilled from the bottom up. They drilled a thirty-six-inch hole for air into the coal mines. That was a very interesting rig, to say the least.

We unloaded the bits and other things we brought and then headed back down the highway toward Texas. We were somewhere in the Cumberland Mountains and stopped at a roadside store. As we walked into the little country store, we saw a girl putting up a bottle of water on a shelf. My dad said to her, "Hey you better watch out. The revenuers will get you for hiding moonshine that way." There were two guys we didn't see in the store, and when my dad said that, they turned around, and we could see their badges and guns.

They said, "That's no laughing matter in these parts. There is more shining going on now than thirty years ago." They were what were known back in those days as G-Men. My dad said he was just making a joke, and we were sorry. They just laughed and said they saw the Texas plates on the truck and knew we were not from around there. We headed on down the road and stopped for gas somewhere around a place I think was called Carrollville.

A black kid about twenty was filling up the truck, and my dad asked him where we could get some moonshine.

This kid put his hands on his hips and said, "There ain't no shining going on in this here place, 'cause we done got us an elected sheriff here in this county, and he don't allow no shining to be going on round here."

"Sorry that we asked," we said. Then we went into the little station, got a Coke and candy bar, and stood around for a few minutes having our little snack.

As we were walking back out to the truck, the black kid followed us, and as we got to the truck, he asked, "Y'all from Texas?"

"Yes," we said, and then he looked around and said, "Y'all come back about ten tonight, and I'll load this truck for five dollars a gallon, get you all the shine yous can carry."

"We can't be here that long," and told him we had to get on down the road back to Texas.

He waved at us as we left, and we stopped next in Memphis to gas up again. My dad asked about some moonshine again, and this time, the guy said, "Sure, how much do you want?"

"Oh, just a quart will do," and he sold us a quart of some stuff that looked like water in a fruit jar for five bucks.

We crossed the bridge over the Mississippi River and were headed across Arkansas when my dad pulled the jar out and asked me if I wanted to try a shot of this fine stuff. "Sure," I said and took a big swallow from the fruit jar. It went down smooth, just like it was water, and didn't taste bad either. When the stuff hit the bottom of my stomach, it caught fire, and the next breath I took, I lost sight of the road. I thought, wow this is some wild juice in that jar. My dad just smiled and said that he figured it to be pretty good stuff.

ᑕᔆ᠊Chapter Seven᠊ᕊᑐ

The next morning, my dad and I headed for Farmington, New Mexico, for what was really me checking on whether or not El Paso Natural Gas Company was ever going to call me or not. We got to Robert West's house in Bloomfield, which is twelve miles from Farmington. The next morning, while they did whatever, I planned to go into Farmington and check with El Paso.

I went into town the next morning and got to the El Paso main office about nine-thirty. When I walked into the main office, the girl at the reception desk asked who I was while dialing a number on her phone.

"Thomas West," I said, and she looked up at me and slammed the phone back down.

She said, "Who did you say you were, and where are you from?"

"I'm Thomas West, and I'm from Amarillo, Texas," I answered.

She said, "Please stay right there," and grabbed a piece of paper that was on her desk and headed down the hall. In just a minute, she came back, followed by a slightly balding guy about forty, and she sat back down at her desk. The guy walked up to me holding the same piece of paper the receptionist had, smiled, shook my hand, and said, "Follow me." When we got to his office, we sat down, and he held up the piece of paper and showed it to me. He said the receptionist was dialing your phone number in Amarillo, Texas, to ask you if you wanted to go to work for the production engineering department here with El

Paso, and you walked in while she was dialing your number. "That is too wild for explanation, so do you want to go to work for the production department?"

"Sure, when do I start?"

We went through all the bull crap that one goes through and went and talked with the manager of the production department. All the paperwork and seeing their doctor and all that and I was hired. They told me they wanted me to be here the day after Labor Day, and I told them that would be great and I would be there.

We went back to Amarillo, and we started getting everything ready to move to Bloomfield, New Mexico. I also rented a house which was next door to my cousin Robert and Carol West who was the son of my dad's younger brother Ike West. Before I told the people I would take the house, I asked Robert if they would mind us living next door to them. They were happy about this, and we went back to get our things.

I had lived in the house in Amarillo for almost two years and we knew the neighbors fairly well, but not everyone on the street. About a week before we moved, we had a yard sale, and some of the people we had not met came to the sale. One woman from across the street and down three houses came over to look around at the things we were selling. When I saw this woman, I thought I remembered her. She said her name was Emma and told me where she lived. I then asked, "Are you Emma Hammett from Borger?"

Her eyes lit up, and she said, "Yes, I am. Are you Tommy West that lived over on the next street in the country club addition in Borger?"

"Yep, it's me," I said. Her dad was the pro at the golf course I played at while in Borger. Emma and I had a thing going for a very short time, once upon a time, a long time ago.

This was the first time I had seen her in about ten years. We stood there and talked about old times for an hour.

The next day, I was out in the yard, and she came out of her house. When she saw me, she waved and walked over to talk to me again. We stood on the sidewalk and talked for an hour. My wife was not home. She and the boys were at Morse with her folks. Emma and I talked about everything under the sun. Finally, she said that she and her husband were okay, but why didn't she and I get to know each other again, like a long time ago? This was another offer I turned down. We're moving tomorrow, I told her, and this kind of ended the affair before it could get started.

The next day, we moved to New Mexico, and the next seven years were going to be interesting, to say the least. I started work for El Paso on the seventh of September of 1970 and the crew in the production office was the most unique group of guys I have ever been around in my life. No one used their names. Everyone had a nickname and mine the first day became Tex. It stayed all the time I worked for El Paso. Well, everyone had a nickname except the fellow I worked with, come to think of it. That's because his first name was Guy. The production department was different than all other departments in the area. All departments with El Paso in Farmington were part of the San Juan division except the production group. We were a home office division directly out of El Paso, Texas. El Paso was one of the biggest employers in northwestern New Mexico. The San Juan division was made up of field departments of which there were seven. There were four pumping stations, I think, and then there was Heavy Maintenance, Welding Warehouse, Transportation, Well Test, and Engineering— Production Engineering. The Production department, as I said, was not in the San Juan Division, so we were treated differently from all the rest. El Paso had about 4,500 wells in the division around the northwest part of the state and some in southern Colorado.

The production department covered all the wells in the San Juan division when it came to fixing problems or running the production of the wells.

We had two trucks that did most of the repair work on wells and just about anything the engineers wanted us to do. We also had guys that took care of production in a given area and there were seven of these. I was assigned to work with Guy Evans on truck 506, and the other truck was 407. These numbers were for each unit the company had in the division. There were over 300 units in all the divisions, and to talk to someone in their truck, you would use the unit number like 506.

The two trucks that did all the work on wells had two people in each. Guy and Tex in 506 and Swamp Rat and the Kid were in 407. The fellow who was the manager of production was known by more than one name. He was one of the most unique people I have ever met. His real name was Robert Horvath, but his nicknames were Captain Zero, Zero, Bruno, Horse Shit, and some others I have forgotten about. Bruno and Zero were the most common ones that were used every day.

We would get to work at 7:00 AM and get our work tickets about 7:30 to 7:45 each morning. Then, we would go to the warehouse to get the supplies we needed to do these jobs. After that we usually would go to the Triangle Café in Bloomfield to drink coffee before heading out to the fields to do the jobs. Each of the seven fields had an engineer and a technician who would put in the work orders when they needed some work done on a well in their field.

I realize this is more information about the operation of the San Juan Division of El Paso Natural Gas Company than you might need to live a long and fruitful life, but you will see the reason as you continue reading about how unique this time period of seven years with the gas company really was.

It will take some time to explain all about the evolution of the production department from 1970 to 1977. In September of '70, there were three engineers and three techs for all seven fields, but as production problems got bigger, it grew to seven engineers and seven techs in a couple of years. The two trucks that did all the work stayed at two because we were so darn good we could take care of all seven, just like we did the three in 1970. As things grew, the people on the maintenance trucks were promoted to techs in the fields. Some of these fields were over sixty miles from Farmington, so some of the techs lived in field houses like Governador, Lindrith, Librook, and so on. The techs that were closer to town lived in Bloomfield, Farmington, or Aztec. These three towns were in a triangle of about ten miles.

I started out as a helper on truck 506 with Guy who was the one that ran the truck. The Swamp Rat and the Kid ran truck 407. We got the work tickets from Captain Zero and, as I stated, did what we did each day. Sounds simple enough, but as I said we were very good at what we did. We had a lot of time to do some things that would get the company sued weekly in the 21st century. Sexual harassment and harassment of all kinds was happening daily by everyone in production engineering. Most of these foul deeds were done by the production truck people.

About two weeks after I started with the company, Guy and I came back to the shop in the afternoon. The guys on 407 were putting small parts into a cardboard box that had been rigged above the front door of the office. The more we laughed about who the box would fall on, the more parts were put into the box. Finally, Zero showed up and thought something was up so he went in the back door of the shop. At about the same time, another person drove into the parking lot that I have not mentioned yet. His name was Gordon Sitzsinger, but he was known as Shitslinger in the company. I worked there for seven years and never found out what Shitslinger's job was except to find ways to get in everyone's way as often as he could.

Shitslinger came in the front door and the now heavy box fell on his head. On his knees, rubbing his head and almost saying some very foul language (Shitslinger was a Mormon Bishop, we think), he wanted to know why Zero could not control his men. Zero said, "Don't worry, it wasn't meant for you." We all retreated to the shop and blamed it on the cleaning people.

We did things like put pipe dope on the door handles to Zero's office, put a live rattlesnake in Zero's desk drawer, and hooked up a loudspeaker to Zero's phone so all the calls could be heard two blocks down the street. We set off a fire extinguisher in the restroom while a poor soul was in there doing his business.

One of the techs had the handle of Mother, and for seven years when he came into the office in the morning, he always had the same greeting for everyone. We would say as one voice, 'Good morning, Mother,' and his reply would be, 'Screw you sons-of-bitches.' Mother carried a lunch box that covered half the seat in his truck that his butt wasn't sitting on. We always wanted to see what he hauled in there, but he never gave anyone the chance to look.

November came around, and I was learning how to do the job quite well and all the talk was about deer hunting. Finally, the day before hunting season was upon us and we carried our hunting rifles with us to sight them in one last time before the season opened. This was northwestern New Mexico, and about half the territory was very good for hunting Bambi. Truck 506 had a job just to the north of Bloomfield, and Guy and I saw five or six Antelope about 700 yards away, going up a hill. Guy stopped and took out his 308 and shot at one of the

Antelope and missed by twenty yards low. He said, "You try to hit one at this distance with your 30-06."

"Sure," I said. Just looking beside the barrel, I raised it up to where I thought it would get to the antelope that were now 800 yards away. I fired, and the lead animal dropped like a rock. "What a shot," he said, "Now what do we do?"

"Go get the damned thing," I said, and we drove for twenty minutes trying to get to him. When we got there, the Antelope had been hit in the spine at the front shoulders and was still alive, except his back legs didn't work very well. We administered the Coup de Gras and we proceeded to dismantle the critter. He was very tasty, I might add.

I have always loved little animals. They usually taste great and are very filling. Sort of like Miller beer, only better.

We got hunting season over with and yes, I did kill Bambi and ate him as well. In fact, I shot two deer in five minutes on the first day of the season. The first deer was on purpose. The second one was in self-defense. I headed back to camp to get the little rig that we used to transport the deer when I heard a shot from behind me. I was about halfway up this hill in the middle of a big clump of oak brush. I looked around when I heard the shot and saw a buck deer running right at the oak brush I was in the middle of. This trail was not very wide. I leaned back as far as I could because I could see the deer had no idea I was there. When he passed me in the bushes, I shot him with the barrel of the gun less than two inches from his side. The blast burned the hide where he was shot, and the deer, thank God, jumped the other way. The fellow who shot at the deer came running up and said, "Wow, what a shot."

"Yeah," I said, "you skin this one, and I'll go get another one." We both laughed at the wild events and went and got the little rig to haul the deer.

One day it had snowed about eight inches, and we had a work ticket in what was called the Angel Peak Bad Lands. This is an area that even Euell Gibbons could not survive. It is a place where nothing grows, not even a weed. We pulled our truck up beside the Old Man's truck to talk a minute and up drove Shitslinger. He got out to go potty, and we did the same thing. We had left the coffee shop thirty minutes earlier, and it was time to go. Shitslinger, as I already said, was a Mormon. Just then, the Old Man said, "The snow looks cold." Shitslinger answered that it's also deep.

The Old Man looked at me and said, "Well, I guess that is why he is a Mormon bishop. He makes three tracks in the snow." (You figure it out).

One summer, while working on a well we saw a lizard, a big lizard called a Mountain Boomer. They are about ten to twelve inches long when grown, and this one was large. They are brightly colored and with an emerald-colored head. Well, we caught this creature and put him in a peanut can and closed the lid. We took him back to the office with us that afternoon, and when we got there, the Old Man was leaning back against the wall, sitting in a folding chair. I had the peanut can and walked over to the Old Man and asked, "You want a peanut?" and opened the lid. The big lizard was a little unhappy being copped up in there all afternoon and landed on the shirt of the Old Man. They were eyeball to eyeball, and I in all my life never saw a person fall so far with his ass being only two feet off the floor. He looked like an Olympic Gymnast doing the floor exercise. It was a gold medal performance, too. The whole office laughed so hard we almost were sick from laughing.

One of the techs smoked a pipe, and one day, he had left his can of Prince Albert on the table in the office. We never passed up a chance like this while I worked there. We gathered some deer pellets, crushed them up, and replaced the tobacco with the deer pellets. Heck, it even looked like Prince Albert. Well, anyway, when this genius got back to the office, the can was right where he had left it that morning. He grabbed it up and commenced to load his pipe. When he lit it and took a long puff, he started turning up his nose and sniffing the air. "Smells like shit," he said, and three or four of us said at the same time, "Yes, and I believe it is shit." He never left his tobacco in the office again, ever.

We bought five acres between Farmington and Bloomfield and built quite a nice place. We had a modular home. I built a two-car garage and a barn with corrals and nice fences. We enjoyed living out there. Life was not too bad. We made okay money and the kids were starting school. El Paso was a pretty good company to work for.

The first September after I started working for El Paso, I got a vacation. We loaded up the family and went back to the Texas Panhandle to see the folks. I had talked to a friend of mine about buying his boat for about two years. When we got back home, I went to see him about the boat. He sold the thing a week before I got there. Just my luck, so we went to Amarillo, and I bought a new Honda 175 motorcycle. This bike was half dirt bike and half road bike. They called them dual-purpose bikes. It was okay on the road, not much power, and shitty in the dirt, too heavy. I rode the thing for a month and traded it for a Yamaha 250 race motorcycle. It had lots of power if you could keep the thing wound up tight enough. I was fairly new to riding in the sand of northwestern New Mexico, so this motorcycle was hard to ride. I traded it off after two months and got a 360 CZ. Now, this was a dirt bike. It would do just about anything you wanted it to do. It was big and powerful and could throw your ass in a New York second. It was also a blast to ride and ride it I did. I learned to ride the dirt fairly well over the next six months.

I rode with guys I knew from Bloomfield, and we rode a lot for the next six months. When Frank Johnson sold his big bike, I thought I might sell mine and get a smaller one to just play around with. I took my bike to the Aztec racetrack in May 1972 and was going to try to sell it there. The fellow at the gate said, "You will have more luck selling this if you race it." I thought about that for at least three seconds and said, "Sure, why not." I went home, got my riding stuff, and went back to the track to become a motorcycle racer.

This racetrack was set up for AMA-type TT scrambles. That is one-half of a quarter-mile oval and the other half sort of like a motocross with turns and a jump.

I lined up at the starting line in the open class qualifier and looked at the twelve other motorcycles and wasn't sure I could compete with them. But I wasn't there to compete with them; I was there to sell my scooter, right? The green flag went up, and off we went. I was dead last. I just rode around the track the first three laps and looked at the crowd and something inside me said to turn it on and try to win this thing. I cranked the right-handle grip and went for it. By the tenth lap, I was in second place, but I couldn't catch the rider in the front. He was good and had a faster motorcycle than I had. My bike was geared for the dirt riding I had done, and it didn't have the top speed to catch the leader.

All three qualifiers and the semi-main and the main event I finished in second place behind the Husky rider. When it was over, they were handing out the prize money. Yes, it was an AMA pro race, and I said to the Husky rider, "I'll be back next week and a lot faster, so be ready."

My first race and I was talking trash to the winner. Now, what was I going to do? Well, I went home and started working on my CZ. I changed the gearing so it would run about fifteen miles per hour faster. Put on new brakes and changed tires, and when the next Friday came around, I went back to the race track, not to sell my bike, but to kick some Husky ass. Besides, now I am a professional motorcycle racer, and the checkered flag was all I could see. I wanted to win and show others, as well as myself, that I was a winner. I think everyone wants to win at something. It's what we do here in America. We are winners at just about everything and every sport and every war we get into.

Here is why I wanted to win, and I'm oversimplifying this scenario to make my point. We here in America started this country by winning the War of Independence. We had some guys who were brilliant and wrote a constitution that was, and still is, the best guide for a country in the history of man. Our country, America, was built by people kicking ass for over two hundred years. We kicked the English in the Revolutionary War twice. We have beaten them all ever since. Some might disagree about this, but not if they are very smart.

I was starting to see changes in the way most things were being done, and I was not paying attention. It's not because I'm not smart enough to look, but it was because I was too caught up in life. I got an advertisement in the mail to write to this place for a test to see if I would qualify for Mensa. I sent off for the test and took it the morning we left on vacation. About a month later I received a letter from Mensa stating that I had an IQ in the upper two percent of the world's population. It also stated if I wanted to join their society, I would need to complete the application and take another test because I was on the percentage line that Mensa accepted for membership. I didn't bother; I already knew where I stood. I was very happy just where I was at the time.

I, as I have said and will state, am not very political or politically correct. I am not really very happy with the way this country has become in the 21st century. I have and always will

121

call a spade a spade. As a whole, this country has, from time to time, become very stupid in its way of thinking. We got stupid in 1860; we had that problem in WWI and got very, very dumb at the end of WWII. We, as a country have become lazy and only want to get by and never ahead. We could have kicked the ass of the world in WWII, but we let someone else get in the last kick.

But let's get totally philosophical for a little while. Since the USA got started, it's been winning with capitalism and getting more politically correct with each passing year. Let's start with capitalism in its purest form. We needed it; we invented it and then made a business selling it to the world. For the most part, it was invented by the white race that came from Europe or invented by Europeans who stayed in Europe. The modern times did not evolve out of Africa or Asia. It was not invented by Africans or Asians although the Asians sure could copy it rather nicely.

Thomas Jefferson said that all people were created equal; they were not. Maybe in a perfect world, all people should be treated equally, but they are not and were never created equal. Anyone who believes that is blind and stupid.

If the slaves from Africa were not sold here in America, most of them would still be running around the forest naked, throwing spears at the animals and each other. The Native American red man would be sitting in front of his teepee today just as he did 300 years ago without what the whites have invented in the last 200 years.

If this pisses you off, that's too bad. It is true, and the truth can't be changed. Oh, I know some have come up with a few little ideas after getting through schools that were invented by whites.

I've said all this to let you know how I feel about why we want to win every time we play or do anything in this country. This country was started by winning, so let's not get stupid and lazy in the 21st century and throw it all away. I'm too old to start over completely.

Back to my racing—I got to the racetrack with some friends and got ready for the first heat race. We lined up on the starting line and I knew I was the fastest thing out there. When the first heat race was over, everyone else knew I was the fastest thing out there. I was almost a complete lap ahead of the rider in second place, and by the way, it was the Husky rider. The other heat races were the same, and I easily won the main event. Now, not only was I a professional motorcycle racer, but a darn good one, too. My wife said to me when it was over that she was glad I didn't break my leg. Well, that did a lot to help my confidence to continue racing.

I got an offer about a month later to sell my CZ motorcycle for just about what I had paid for it. The cost of repairs was just about equal to the amount of money I was winning. Yes, I was even better than I thought I was at racing the bikes, but this was not getting me anywhere. I was risking a broken leg or something worse and not getting much money after repairs, so I took the offer and sold the CZ. But, if you boil it all down, I did it to prove to myself I could win.

I bought a 360 MX Yamaha race bike and it was a lot more dependable as a racer. I say that because it would start every time I wanted it to. It was as fast as the old bike and easier to ride. I hauled the thing all the way to the Texas Panhandle to race it at a new track. The day of the race the temperature was 104 with not much wind. It was hot and with no shade. I ran about twenty laps of practice and had to lie in front of my car and have Roger pour water over me to cool off. Wearing all leather pants and a shirt in heat at 104 is not fun, but I was going to win, and that's all I cared about.

The first race started, and in the open class, there were about fifteen racers. By the second lap, I was in front, and by the last lap, I was so far out in front I rode across the finish line on the back wheel, waving at the crowd. This was going to be easy. Not. In the second race, I was in the lead when we got to the first corner, and in the second corner, poo-poo hit the fan. As I backed off the gas to turn the bike, the engine stayed at full power. I had no control at all. The thing wouldn't slow down. I hit the kill button and crashed. I tried to get it going again, but nothing worked. I got back to the pits and took the carburetor apart and found that a little keeper spring had broken that would only cost $2.00. Yes, I was mad because I had driven 500 miles and won the first race, then a two-dollar part broke, which ruined the whole weekend. I darn near died from the heat as well. I lost almost nine pounds of weight from the heat that day.

I also bought a smaller Honda, reworked it, and started winning at motorcycle trials competitions. In fact, I won every trial I entered but one. The next thing I did was to start racing with a sponsor. This was better than using my own bike and breaking two-dollar parts and getting very mad about it.

The Maico dealer gave me a new 450 cc Maico, and I raced it for a time. I was not one of the racers who said if something breaks, I'll be back next time.

I went to a European hill climb which is a race up a mountain, and even after falling off at over fifty miles per hour and getting up and back on the damned thing, I finished third in the open class. At the end of the day, I realized I was really thirty-two years old and that the wreck hurt like hell. The thing that bothered me the most was I got beat by two kids who weren't even twenty years old. I did the only smart thing I could do. I quit. Yep, I told the sponsor he could have his motorcycle back and to find a kid with no brains and a full-throttle and get him to ride for you.

I went home and, within two weeks, sold my motorcycles and didn't ride another one except around the block a couple of times when someone I knew asked me too. It was time to move on in my life and see what else I could get into. This had been just a hobby to me because I kept my full-time job with El Paso. At the age of thirty-two, I thought I needed to quit taking a chance of breaking my neck racing motorcycles.

In December 1972, my dad and mom were living in Farmington as well, and dad, being retired, did more than most people do when they are working for a living. He sold cars, drove a truck, and hauled special loads for people he had gotten to know. My dad was not one to sit still for very long anywhere. Just before Christmas of that year, he called me one afternoon as I got home from work and asked me if I was off for the next couple of days, and I told him I was. He said the candy factory at the west end of town had a small load of candy bowls that needed to be delivered to Las Vegas, Nevada. "You want to go and help drive?"

"Sure," I said, "When are you going?"

"Now," he said. "You ready to go?"

We headed for Las Vegas and drove all night to get there. We parked at the Mint in downtown Las Vegas about 4:30 in the morning and I walked into the first casino I had ever seen. Wow, this was quite a sight, slot machines ringing; this was really a cool place, I thought as we went into the main casino. My dad said he needed to walk across the street to the Golden Nugget and cash a check, and he asked what I was going to do. I told him I would stay here and look around for a while. Dad said we would eat breakfast here in the Mint. He left and I started walking around looking at all the machines and table games. It was very early in the morning, and not many people were gambling. Workers were cleaning and vacuuming the carpet, and a bunch of guys were taking coins out of the slot machines and loading them on carts flanked by security guards.

I got to the first craps table I had ever seen, and there was this old man playing craps by himself. There were two men standing next to some slot machines, watching this old man shoot the dice. I stood at the end of the table for a minute just looking when the old man asked me "Want to play young man?"

"Sir," I told him, "I don't know how to play this game; this is my first time in Las Vegas."

The old man, wearing a long coat and little black beret, said, "Well, get your money out, and I will teach you how to play craps."

I pulled a twenty-dollar bill out of my wallet, and as I gave it to the dealer for chips, I looked at the old man and asked, "Sir, are you Groucho Marx?"

The old man looked up and said, "Well, yes, I am Groucho Marx. Who are you?"

I told Groucho my name and where I was from, and he slowly walked up to me and stuck out his hand. He asked me if I was here for the Christmas holidays, and I told him we were here to deliver some candy bowls to a shopping center. Well, Groucho taught me how to shoot craps, and I won ten dollars. I was thrilled, and after about thirty minutes, I said I should go find my father. I thanked Groucho, cashed in my chips, and headed across the street to the Golden Nugget.

I found Dad playing blackjack at a table in the Nugget, and he asked me what I had been doing. I said, "I have been playing craps with Groucho Marx."

My dad jerked his head around and said, "Who?"

"Groucho Marx," I said and pointed in the direction of the Mint across the street.

Dad got up from the table and said, "Show me."

I knew this was going to be hard for him to believe because Groucho Marx had been one of the biggest stars in Hollywood for many, many years. We walked back across the street to the Mint, and sure enough, when we got to the craps table, Groucho looked at me and said, "Tommy, is this your dad?"

"Yes, sir," I answered. Groucho stuck out his hand to shake, and I wasn't sure if my dad could believe what was happening. We stood there and talked with Groucho for a few more minutes and then went to the second-floor coffee shop for breakfast.

That afternoon, while Dad was taking a nap in the hotel room, I decided to go looking around the strip in Vegas. I drove to the Aladdin and then to Caesars Palace to check out that place. I pulled into the parking lot on the north side of Caesars and a gray Rolls Royce parked next to me. A girl got out of the Rolls just as I was getting out of the pickup truck.

This girl was wearing a full-length Mink coat and had on more diamonds than a Zales jewelry store. We got to the door of Caesars, and I, being a gentleman from Texas opened the door for this woman. Now, on a scale from one to ten, this lady would score about sixteen. She was flawless in every way, from head to toe. I walked in behind her and started looking around. Caesars was the most incredible place I had ever seen, with a ship in water next to a bar. Wow, I thought as I strolled through, gawking at everything. I got back to the bar after walking around for a few more minutes and thought I should drink a beer in this place just to say I had. My eyes were getting adjusted to the light now, and when I sat down on one of the stools at the bar, who was sitting next to me but the knockout gorgeous girl in the mink coat. Everyone in the bar area was talking to this gal and calling her by the name "Mother Goose." She went over to one of the tables where three guys were sitting and started talking to them. I thought I had to ask the bartender about this woman. The bartender said, "Yes, that's Mother Goose, and my young friend, she costs about $1,500 per night." I guess I had a very surprised look on my face, and the bartender then said she is one of the highest-priced hookers in Vegas and she lives in one of the penthouse suites here at Caesars.

"Cool," I said, "thanks for the information. I'll keep her in mind if I need some company tonight." At that price, I couldn't afford two minutes, and that would maybe be too long.

We spent the night and unloaded most of the candy bowls, but we had about twenty of the candy bowls left when we headed home the next morning. We drove to the Grand Canyon and stopped just long enough to say I had been there. We headed out across the country toward New Mexico and saw a group of Navajos beside the road with jewelry for sale. I became an Indian trader that day. I showed some of the women the candy bowls and wound up trading candy bowls worth about eight dollars for fifty dollars worth of jewelry. Good trade on our part and the Indian ladies looked like they were happy about the trade as well.

What I got into next wasn't nearly as exciting as racing bikes, but fun anyway. I bought a Baja Ford Bronco by Bill Strope. It was red, white, and blue with a flat black hood. It had the engine and tranny for the job but lacked a lot in handling. I added off-road shocks, big tires, and a pressure system for the fuel, and it worked just about as good as a stock Jeep. We ran all over the hills with the thing and had a good time. The bad part was it only got eight miles per gallon of gas.

That fall during deer season, on the first Sunday morning, things were calm, and the weather was very nice for November. I was getting up and was going to go over to get some coffee when we heard something hit the house. It sounded like someone hit the house siding with a baseball bat. Cody was standing in the hallway and yelling that someone just made a hole in the wall of the bathroom. I ran into the bathroom, saw a bullet had come through the shower doors, and hit the wall about three feet above the sink. Cody said he had climbed up on the counter to get some water to drink, and just as he jumped to the floor, the bullet hit where he had been just a second ago.

I told Jeanie to call the police, and I would see if I could find out who shot our house. I grabbed my shotgun, loaded it with buckshot, and took off in my Ford Bronco. I knew from the angle of the holes in the walls the shooter must be down by the river about 600 yards to the south of our house. I saw a parked truck and two guys walking toward the car carrying deer rifles. I got out of the Bronco and asked the guys if they just shot toward the highway at a deer. One of the guys got very smart with me and said it was none of my business. I grabbed my shotgun and put a shell into the chamber. I told both guys I ~~would~~ will kill someone in about two seconds if someone ~~didn't~~ doesn't tell me who just shot their gun. The one who got smart started to raise his rifle, and I put the shotgun on my shoulder. "I will kill you if you move your gun. Now that shot hit my house."

The other fellow very quickly said, "I shot two times at a deer. Was anyone in your house hurt?"

I told him, luckily, "No, but there is a lot of damage to my house." Just then, two sheriffs' cars pulled up, and the Mexican standoff was over. The one fellow who did the shooting paid us over $700.00 for the damage to our house, and I think the police took his hunting rifle and didn't give it back.

About the same time all this took place, we decided to sell our place in the country and, if it sold maybe move back to Texas. My company, El Paso, was becoming sort of a dead-end in the late 1970s, and the family, mainly Jeanie, didn't really like New Mexico.

I was beginning not to like things here either. We belonged to a water users association and it was run by a president and board of directors. In the mid-1970s, the valves and meters for this type of service were in short supply. Adding water meters was not easy and one had to wait for at least six months to get a meter. When I bought the land in 1972, we purchased two shares in the Water Association because my dad also put a house on the property. Mother and Dad had moved and sold their house. So, we decided to sell two and one-half acres of our land to a guy to put a house on it. I sold him the land, and we found there were no water meters available for his land. I told the fellow I would hook him up to our water line until a meter became available. This was fine with him, and we put in the lines, and he was happy about it. The association was not as happy about the water line as we were. They called me and wanted to know how this guy could put in a new home with water and no meter. I explained to them that I had two shares for the water, and until he could get a meter, I hooked him up to my water line. They told me I couldn't do that and they would come and pull my water meter and shut the water off at to my place. They didn't check to see if I had two shares. It was well within my rights to have two houses on the water meter if I wanted them.

The next afternoon, as I was arriving home from work, a backhoe was sitting on in the edge of my driveway, starting to dig where my water meter was located. I asked the driver what he was doing. He said he was instructed by the president of the water users association to dig my meter up for breaking the rules of the association. I told him this was bullshit and to hold on for just a minute that I would be right back. I went into the house and came back out with a 30-30 Winchester and aimed the gun at the operator of the backhoe. I told him if the bucket of your backhoe touches my land, I will kill you. I told him to get the hell off my place and don't ever come back. I think he knew I wasn't kidding, and he hauled ass as fast as the tractor would run. I then called the county and had a judge give me a restraining order to stop the association from any further action against my water rights. They then found I owned two shares in the association and didn't do anything else. I went to see the president a few days later and found out he was putting a subdivision in on his land and wanted all the water meters he could get his hands on. I told him that I was not sure how much trouble you want for yourself, but if you continued like this, I ~~would~~ will do all I can to stop you one way or the other. I got with some of the other members and got enough people to call an election and vote this crook out of office.

Well, our place finally sold in the early summer of 1977, and we did decide to move back to the Texas Panhandle. In mid-July, we loaded up, and back to Texas, we went. We bought a new house in Dumas, Texas, and I went to work for a cattle hauling company in Cactus, Texas, that hauled fat cattle for Swift, the meat processing company.

We went to the feedlots and picked up cows and hauled them to become steaks and hamburgers. I don't have a problem with this because I am a member of PETA (People Eating Tasty Animals). This was not too bad, and I kind of liked it until one day, I got this phone call from a guy who wanted to talk to me about the company I worked for. I said sure and we met and had dinner at a very nice café and when he told me why he called this meeting I wasn't sure what to do. He said he was working for a company that had all the driver contracts for our company as well as the drivers at Iowa Beef in Amarillo and wanted me to manage both. I asked why they wanted me and how they heard of me. He gave me a story about how they checked me out and I was who they wanted to manage these operations for them. I told him I would talk to my wife and get back to him the next day.

The next morning, very early, the manager of the company that did all the maintenance for the trucking company called me and asked me to come out to his office. He wanted to talk in person, not on the phone. I got in the car and drove out to his office. He asked me if a guy from the driver contracting company had offered me the job as manager for both Swift and Iowa Beef. I told him that was correct and how did he know of the offer. He wouldn't tell me how he knew, but he pulled out the Wall Street Journal and handed it to me. He showed me the front page which was a story about the company that had made me the offer last evening.

To start with, the guy who said he was the finance officer for this company was not. He was a mafia hitman from New York City and had a record as long as your arm. He had never been convicted of much but had been suspected in at least two murders and many other things just about as bad. The mafia family in New York at that time was very well known.

That made my mind up really quick, and when I called him, I gave him a line of shit to explain all the reasons I couldn't take them up on their offer. After about another week, I got the idea that turning them down and staying on as a driver for the same company was not going to work out.

Once again, I needed to find another way to make a living. I put in an insurance office in Dumas selling mostly homeowners and car insurance. Dumas was growing, and the insurance business was not too bad. I also did applications for a mortgage lending company out of Houston, Texas, for fifty bucks an application. I was making a living, but with the entire work taking place in the evening I was not really happy. With one son playing baseball and the other taking karate, I was never there for the games or contests.

I started playing racquetball,-some and one day, the president of the First State Bank of Dumas asked me to play him. We played and had a very good time. As we were walking to the locker room, he asked me how I liked the insurance business. I told him I did, with the exception of the evenings that took away from my family. He said he understood and he might have a solution to my problem. He told me to come by the bank the next day, and we would discuss it over coffee.

The next morning, I went into the bank. Weston and I sat down in his office, and he got right to the point. He said he had been watching me at the Lions Club and really liked what he saw. He told me his installment loan officer was leaving and offered me the job. I didn't know what to say and told him I would talk it over with my family and get back to him in a day or two.

That afternoon I had some business at the bank where my wife's family had done business for many years. The First State Bank of Stratford was about twenty-five miles north of Dumas. I sat down in the office of the president of the bank and, in the conversation, told Harold about the offer Weston had made me. Harold didn't bat an eye before he asked me if I was interested in banking. I told him I didn't know much about the business, but I would look at it because of the family thing. Harold just smiled and said, "Tom, I'm going to make you the same kind of offer Weston made you, but one he can't match. You interested enough to hear about it?"

I said, "Yes, I was," and he did make me an offer that the bank in Dumas couldn't match.

ᏪᏬᎧ᠑Chapter Eight᠎᠍᠎᠑

I took the offer from the bank at Stratford and got rid of the insurance agency in Dumas. I had a month-to-month lease where my office was, so it was not really a very big deal to divest myself of the agency. I was in an office next door to a place called Mr. Johns. It was a clothing store, and the owner was John Waggoner from Perryton, Texas. His wife was Diann Hanner, who I had dated for half the time I was in high school. We had not seen each other for over fifteen years. I went into the clothing store to check out what they had and found out these were people I had known for a very long time. I knew Diann for a long time—not her husband. We talked a lot over the next few months but never really talked about what she wanted to say to me. I didn't know this until many years later. I will get to that in another chapter, maybe. I think I knew what she wanted to say. We were together for only a short time, and once again, when her family came to town. She was still very much in love with me. This too I might get into later in this writing.

Anyway, I went to work for the First State Bank of Stratford, Texas. This was one of the most unusual banks in the country. They had a brick lobby and handwoven carpet in the offices and a gun collection in the bank as well. We had paintings on the walls by Maynard the artist that did most of the United States Duck Stamps for hunting. These paintings were about $200,000 each, and we had about ten of them in the bank. This bank was run by a man who started with the bank as the janitor when he was only nineteen years old. He worked as a teller and did about everything you can do in a bank over the next twenty-five years and wound up as the president of the bank. He was also the best bank president I think I ever saw. He knew how to run a bank and was the best guy I ever worked for.

The job came with a membership to the Stratford Country Club, and I played golf, so this was going to be great. Harold said that the bank closes at three in the afternoon, and if you were still there at four in the afternoon, you were not doing your job right. You should be either on the golf course or, heaven forbid, the tennis court by four every day. This sounded great and I chose the golf course, of course.

Within a couple of months of starting the job in Stratford I was still living in the new house we had built in Dumas and driving back and forth every day. Not too bad by some standards but I didn't like the time it took. One day, I met, just by chance, a guy who owned a picture studio in Dumas. I told him I worked for the bank in Stratford. He said, "Are you here in Dumas shopping?"

"No, I live here and work in Stratford." He told me he lived in Stratford and worked in Dumas.

"Well, how about trading houses? It would help us both."

We looked at his home and he ours and decided we would get the best end of the trade. His home was custom built with marble floors and beautiful landscaping and 800 square feet bigger than our new tract house in Dumas. We traded even. This was because Dumas was about 15,000 people and growing, while Stratford was 1,900 people and just about the same today. Not much changes in the little farming towns in the upper Texas Panhandle.

Things went really well there in Stratford. The job was good, and I was learning the banking business. The golf course was okay as well, and I played at least five days per week. Yep, we had the American dream by the tail, and the kids were doing great in school. The job was getting better the more I learned. Hell, what more could I ask for except more money, of course. Banking had a lot of clout for an officer but the money was not very good. We had other income from Jeanie's farm, and I would buy and sell a car every so often. Things went fairly smoothly the first year and most of the second year.

We got talked into going to the tennis court one evening and playing that horrible game with another couple. The woman also worked at the bank. I have never been any good at the game of tennis. My mother, on the other hand, was one of the best tennis players in college in Oklahoma. I think she always wanted us to learn to play tennis, but we never did. My mother was one of a kind and would never say a thing about being disappointed with us not liking tennis.

There we were, hitting the tennis ball back and forth like fools. When I got the chance to smash the ball, I took it. I could see the little tennis ball leaving a mark on the body of my opponent, and I overswung to the point that I hyperextended my left knee and broke it.

Well, crap, here I am, laying on my back in the middle of the tennis court with two EMTs trying to put my left leg into a plastic splint and haul me off. One of the people playing on the next court was the owner of the local newspaper, and being a good reporter, he was standing there watching the whole process of the EMT's misguided efforts to haul away my broken body. Having no microphone and no recording devices handy he held his tennis racket, handle first, in front of my face and said, "Do you have any comment for the press about the game of tennis?"

"Yes, as a matter of fact, I do," and I did, and the fool printed it on the front page of the newspaper the next issue.

LOCAL BANKER BREAKS LEG ON TENNIS COURT SAYS THE GAME SHOULD BE BANNED FOR ANYONE SMARTER THAN A BOX OF ROCKS.

This did not endear me to the local tennis groups around town. If I even drove down the street where the tennis court was, the tennis fools would stick out their tongues or other body parts and say a few choice words. This was really kind of a local joke because the newspaper didn't have that much to write about in the little town of Stratford, so when something like this happened, they really had fun with it.

I was elected to the office of President of the Stratford Lions Club the second year I was there. We had our weekly dinner, and yep, they wanted the new banker to be the president. Hell yeah, and I gladly accepted the job with speech and all.

The doctor told me the best thing for my left leg was to walk a lot every day, so I played golf every afternoon that I could. The leg was now doing fine, and my golf game was getting much better, too.

One morning, the manager of our insurance company, whose offices were next to the bank, came into my office, sat down, and wanted to talk. This was very weird because Bobby only came into the office from Amarillo, maybe once a month. He was the son-in-law of the owner of the bank and didn't normally talk to any of us in the bank. He started off the conversation with, "Do you buy a lot of stock in the market."

"Some," I told him, "Why do you ask?"

"Jimmy was talking with his next-door neighbor this morning over coffee, and T. Boone Pickens told Jimmy something you might be interested in," he said.

"Sure, go ahead," I told him; T. Boone Pickens was Jimmy Whittenburg's next-door neighbor. T. Boone said he was going to sell all his Canadian oil properties for 190 million and announce it in his board meeting this afternoon. "What do you think that will do to his stock?"

"Okay," I said. I got the picture and asked him what he was going to do with this information. He said he was going to buy $250,000 of the stock that morning.

"Great," I told him and thanked him for the information.

As soon as he left my office, I called a broker in Amarillo and asked about buying $10,000 worth of stock options in this company. I also asked whether I could do this over the phone and send the money to him the next day. He put in the order right then and said send the money. I then called the president of another bank I knew, borrowed the $10,000, and said I would sign a note for the money tomorrow. He gave me the loan without another word. I could have borrowed $100,000 on my signature because of my family ties. I also could have called another bank and got another $100,000 the same way that day.

At noon, I went home for lunch and told my wife we were about to make ten years' worth of salary in one month with this little investment. She about crapped right then and there and got mad as hell. I can't argue with someone who doesn't understand much of anything outside of her own little world.

I got so mad when I got back to my office that I called the broker and canceled the stock trade. Well, all that was told to me happened just like they said. The stock went wild over the next thirty days. The $10,000 would have made a net profit of $290,000 that month. What would the $200,000 investment have made? When I figured that one out, I got so mad I just about went ballistic. Why did I even tell her when I was the one who did all the financing in our house anyway? I was too honest and stupid to be that kind of guy, I guess. As I was to learn over the next six months, I was more stupid than I could have ever imagined.

In the early fall, we went hunting at my wife's farm in Morse, Texas. While hunting, I stopped and looked at the well house, which was on her land. It was drilled as a gas well some years earlier, but we had never gotten any royalties from this well or any of the other wells. Her family told me there was no production from these wells. Now I had worked in the oil and gas business for about ten years, and I could read a production chart as well as anyone in the business could. The well had an orifice plate large enough to produce about five million feet per month. The chart was showing production at about that level. This did not compute with the wells not having enough production to even matter.

The next Monday, I called the gas company that owned the well in Oklahoma City. The receptionist gave me to the company lawyer, and when he told me his name, I almost dropped the phone. "This is J.D. Helmes; how can I help you?" he said.

"J. D. Helmes from Spearman?" I asked, and he answered, "Yes. J. D."

I said, "This is Tommy West." He was very glad to hear from me again. I had known J. D. ever since he got out of law school. I explained I wanted to know about this Womble gas well and I gave him the location from the sign I got off the well house. He said he would look into it and call me back.

The next morning, he called me with information about the wells. Not just the one well I asked about but all the ones from the same lease. He told me there were hundreds of thousands of dollars sitting in the lease account. In the five years, no one had given them instructions on dividing up the money to the owners of the lease.

The lease was set up with an override, which gave the owners almost one-quarter of the well's production. This was a hell of a lot of money they were holding. I found out what needed to be done to get the money due to my wife, and the first monthly check was more than I made in the bank all year. These monthly checks would continue for months to come.

As the end of 1979 rolled around, my wife's family had a kind of "here's where we are" meeting at my wife's mother's house. All five of the kids were there as well as their spouses. All eleven of us sat in the dining room and listened to them talk about the farming business and the cattle business and what they had done during the year. They didn't want to hear anything about the banking business or what I had done for the year except one little thing.

I must say what was said to me came as a shock because I have been in this family since 1963 and knew them a couple of years before that. I didn't think I was a complete outsider to their family, but I was to learn differently that day.

About the end of the meeting, without any warning, Jeanie's mother said "Oh, about the gas well royalties we are now getting because of Tom's call to the gas company."

She looked straight at me and, without any hesitation on her part, said to me, "Don't you ever interfere in our family business again."

I wasn't going to take this from someone I had known for almost seventeen years. "It is my wife's money, and I believe we could use it even if none of the rest of you needs it."

Well, this statement from me suppressed Jeanie's mother enough to get the subject changed instantly.

The next thing talked about was whether we wanted to have the yearly dinner at Supkins in Borger next week. We all agreed to have the dinner there as we did almost every year until my wife's little sister-in-law spoke up and said it would not be possible because they have closed up.

I looked at Denna and asked, "Why do you think that they have closed up?"

"Well," she said, "I went by there last Monday, and they were closed, that's why," she said with a smirk. I looked right back at her and answered they have always been closed on Monday ever since they opened their doors in 1951. I had a meeting with a man from Dumas who is buying a franchise from them to put in a barbeque restaurant in Dumas. I have known these people for years, and they would not spend that kind of money on a place that had gone out of business. Oh, and by the way, we can go there and have dinner any day except Monday. This heifer was twenty-three years old and brain-dead from birth. Jeanie's little brother would find out a few years later just how bad she was when she ruined Ronnie's farming business forever. He is now a tractor mechanic somewhere around the Amarillo area, even today, over twenty years later.

On the way home to Stratford that evening, my wife said and very much to my surprise, "I don't want you to ever argue with anyone in my family ever again."

Now, this came as just as big a shock as the statement her mother had made that afternoon. I came unglued and went ballistic. I couldn't help it. Had they all gone mad in one day? I said, "Well, first of all, by God, we needed the damned money that the rest of your rich family evidently doesn't need, and you know damn well that is true. Second, your sister-in-law is an idiot if she thinks the barbeque place is closed and out of business. You know better than that, and why would you take her side in a thing like that." I went off on her for not saying anything to help me all afternoon.

The next weekend, we went to Amarillo, and with the little bit of gas well money we had gotten bought a new Oldsmobile for cash. We also had a great Christmas and put $10,000 in the bank.

Now, I'm not stupid, but I think that back in those days, I was like the big African bird and had my head in the sand. I darn sure wasn't looking around at what was going on in the town as well as in my own house. I was living in the Peyton place of Texas and I didn't pay any attention to it.

There was a guy in Stratford whose wife was screwing every guy that came by. The tennis coach, some of the high school boys, and a lot more. Most of the men in town who had wives working in the bank didn't like me very much, and I really didn't give a darn because I wasn't looking at anything that was going on in our fair little village.

I learned much later most of the men thought I was screwing their wives. I will admit, looking back, most of the gals needed screwing, but I wasn't the one doing the screwing. I was hit on by at least three of them, and I didn't do a thing except act like I wasn't interested at all.

I was then and still am a pretty good guy, and I don't mess around with other men's wives or anyone else, for that matter. But that is a whole other story in itself, and it might be my next book if this one sells and makes me a lot of money.

Harold, the bank president, had a policy on hiring gals to work for him. They had to fail the elbow test to get the job. They put their hands on the back of their heads and if their elbows hit the wall first, they didn't get hired. That might be stretching it a little, but not much.

The country club had a New Year's party at the clubhouse, and of course, we were there. The food was served buffet style and we sat down next to the neighbors from across the street. The woman also worked at the bank. The guy and I were not good friends, but I knew him. We finished eating and were watching the program being put on by some group.

I noticed my wife had slid her hand over on top of the neighbor's leg. Now, this shocked me to the point of not knowing what to do or say. When I looked straight at her very hard and put my lips together in a tight way, she moved her hand. I made some excuse about the food not sitting well on my stomach and told Jeanie I was ready to go home. When we got to the car, I was about as mad as you could get without killing someone.

The next month was not very smooth around the house. I was trying to figure out whether my wife was messing around with this guy or not. The thing I should have figured out was that this is a very small town, and gossip runs rampant. I was not listening and definitely wasn't looking at all the crap going on there.

I had friends we visited with, and some I played golf with, but as I said, I wasn't looking at all the other things going on in this town.

Jeanie had gotten a job keeping books for the Phillips oil wholesaler in Stratford. I didn't know the guy very well, but he went to the same church we did and I did talk with him some. What I'm saying is we were not buddies that played golf or anything. This was a job I thought she needed to get her out of the house and be able to do something productive for her.

The bank wanted me to attend a lending school at the University of Oklahoma starting in early February 1980 and it was now only a week before I would be leaving to go to this school.

I started listening for the first time to all the gossip going on in Stratford. I guess as I'm looking back at this, it must have been that the times were just right for all that was going on in the new Peyton Place. I guess it could have been going on all over the world, but I might have had my head up my ass and wasn't watching or listening to it.

After putting all the pieces together, it kind of pissed me off to think I wasn't looking at anything but what I was doing at the time. I didn't fool around, and I didn't believe that sort of thing affected me because I wasn't doing it.

I knew this sort of thing went on everywhere, but I didn't play the game, and that fact kept me from knowing and seeing what was going on right under my nose.

There were a lot of divorces that year in Stratford, Texas, and I am proud to say I did not cause any of them.

The Sunday I was to leave for Norman, Oklahoma, Jeanie and I had a long talk about some of the crap going on in Stratford. I still didn't see it affecting me at all. Jeanie seemed to know more about some of the stuff than I figured she did.

I got into the new Oldsmobile and drove toward Norman, Oklahoma, and did a lot of thinking on the way there. With all that had gone on the past few months I finally started putting things together, and not just from the past year, but for the last fifteen years. The more I thought on the subject of my marriage, the worse it got. I started putting all the things together that had happened since we were married in 1963. By the time I got to Norman, I think my eyes had finally opened. I got there and had dinner at a café in Norman before going on to the university and getting checked in for the two weeks stay.

I put all my things into the room I was assigned to and was told my roommate, Al Bronsteder, from Michigan, would be coming in on a late plane.

On Monday morning, school started, and after breakfast, we went into a building called the forum. There were 290 bankers in there and we listened to the greetings and started the school. They had some of the group give ideas on certain topics in the afternoon, and speakers took the podium in the forum to present those ideas. No one heard a word of what the first three speakers said because most of the bankers were discussing where they were going to go to drink beer that night.

The fourth speaker was a girl from Wisconsin and very nice looking too. Her way of talking got the attention of everyone in the building. She had command of the place instantly, and I looked at Al and said, "Wow, she's something." I told Al not only was this girl very good-looking, but look at all the people in there; they were hanging onto every word she was saying. I told Al I might just marry her and laughed.

Being the only one at the school with a car, I was elected to run the group's errands, like going to the nearest liquor store. That evening one of the girls from Georgia and I went after some beer for those who gathered in the lounge. The girl was nice looking and was looking at me with I could screw you right now eyes. I almost did right there in the parking lot after getting the beer. We started making out, and then I thought better of things. I already had a mess back home and wasn't looking to add fuel to that fire. So, we ended the making out and delivered the booze to the school.

Yes, I had been having a lot of trouble at home, and I thought a lot about the subject on the drive from Stratford to Norman that Sunday. I guess I was still very pissed about everything going on in my very own Peyton Place. This girl was cute and all, but I wasn't ready to jump into bed with just any girl who was ready to do that. I definitely wasn't at the school to mess around with anyone.

I have had so many chances to screw around. So far, I have turned them all down. Maybe that was why I was so mad about what I guessed was going on in Stratford and probably with my wife.

We all sat around and talked about what we did back home. We got to know each other while drinking beer and watching the Winter Olympics, which had also started the same week. Then another one of the gal bankers started hinting she and I should go screw our brains out. I got out of that suggestion even quicker than the one earlier the same evening. The second one was much more direct about what she wanted to do with the rest of the night.

Tuesday went by and everyone was probably having a fairly good time being away from home and being around a lot of other people with the same type of jobs. I think by Wednesday evening, we were all getting to know some of the people, making friends, and learning something from the school.

ᶜᵕᵖChapter Nine∾

A fter the school ended for the day, groups were sitting around the lobby watching the Olympics or talking or drinking beer. I had been talking to some people when I saw the girl who had given the speech on Monday. She went into a room just down the hall from the lobby, so I walked down there to say hello. I knocked on the wall, for the door was wide open, and when one of the ladies said to come in, I complied.

I introduced myself and they asked me to sit down and stay awhile. We started talking about all sorts of things, and this continued for a couple of hours. Somewhere in one of the conversations, I stopped and said to the gal sitting on the edge of the bed, "Has anyone ever told you that you have very beautiful eyes."

"Yes, a very handsome southern gentleman just told me that," she said with a big smile and laughed. After this statement, I could see something in her eyes saying I would like to know you a little better.

We sat and talked until the other lady gave us the idea, she was tired and wanted to go to bed. I then asked Diana if she would like to go for a little walk. She said she would, even though it was very cold out with some snow still on the grass and parking lots. We put on our coats and headed out into the night, walking and telling each other about ourselves. She was just as interested in me as I was in her. We walked for a couple of hours until neither of us could stand the cold anymore. We stopped at the lobby and played a couple of games of billiards as we talked. I asked her if she wanted to get some coffee somewhere. We got into my car and drove around awhile then got some coffee and drove around until about 5:30 in the morning.

We turned into the parking lot at the dorm, sat there, and talked for another few minutes. Diana said, "I guess I better get back in there so we can get ready to go to the class at 8:00 AM."

I don't quite know why I said it, but I asked her if I could kiss her goodnight. We kissed and kept on kissing for a few minutes and then headed in to get ready for the banking school.

As I got ready, I knew we had started something neither one of us was looking for. Even though we had only known each other for a few hours, I felt like we were falling in love.

We had discussed our lives and the fact we were both married and me with two boys. She had heard me talk a little about some of the things that were going on in my life and she told me some about the problems with her husband.

Neither of us came there to look for someone. This just happened, and we were both very glad it did. That morning in class, we could see something had happened to each of us, and I wasn't sure what we were going to do about it. That evening we had dinner and spent more time just talking and getting to know each other more.

We turned in early because of the lack of sleep the night before, and on Friday evening, we had dinner with Al and Diana's roommate and took in a movie or at least part of a movie. It wasn't that good so we left and went to a nightclub for some drinks and dancing.

We went for a drive after dropping off the other guys back at the dorm and went into Oklahoma City. She had never been to Oklahoma, so I decided to show her some of it. We drove around half the night talking, and somewhere in the middle of the conversation, I just blurted out, "Will you marry me? Diana didn't even hesitate, although she was married, and so was I. She said, "Yes, I will and what do we do now?"

"I'll be darned if I know, but I think we will figure it out somehow."

We spent the rest of the weekend together and went back to the dorm on Monday morning to change for class. We made it through the rest of the week, falling in love more every day. By Friday, when we were to leave, I think we knew what was going to happen to us.

As I drove Diana to the airport, I almost ruined the whole thing for us. I told her even though we feel like we said, we still need to go home and think about what we should do. And we need to take a real good look at what we have. She agreed, and I think she was crying when she got on the airplane. She later told me she cried most of the way back to Milwaukee.

I drove the six hours back to Stratford, trying to think of what to do. By the time I got home, I had the headache of all time.

I didn't say anything to my family about Diana when I got home. I just told them about the school and that I had met a lot of really great people. The next day, we went to Amarillo for the boys to race their MX bikes. On the way back to Stratford, this headache came back with a vengeance. It felt like my head was bursting open.

We had told some friends we would come over that evening to visit. So, headache and all, we went. We were only at the other couple's house for an hour or so when I looked at Jeanie and said, "We need to go because my head is killing me." We got into our car, and the headache went away instantly. I knew what I had to do. I told Jeanie we needed to just drive around for a while and talk about things.

I told her what I thought about the happenings going on in Stratford. I didn't accuse her of anything I just told her there might be things going on I couldn't handle. I didn't accuse her of sleeping with anyone, although after some of the events that happened shortly after we broke up, it would have been justified.

After the two weeks in Oklahoma thinking about what was going on back home, I would have done the same thing even if I had not met someone.

I told her about Diana and finally that I was moving out and would file for a divorce. I don't know and never really tried to find out all the things going on in Peyton Place, Texas, but it was much more than my imagination was telling me. As Like I said, I never asked anyone about what was going on, but I'll bet most of the rumors I heard were true for the most part.

We went home and talked with the boys and told them just about everything they needed to know and I packed up and left.

I went to the bank, let myself in the back door, and called Diana from my office phone. I told her what had happened and that I did really love her very much and wanted to marry her with all my heart.

Diana told her husband somewhat the same thing in the next few days and moved into her parent's house. They only lived about two blocks away from her house.

I had moved into my parent's house in Dalhart, Texas, which was thirty miles from Stratford. The word got around that Jeanie and I had separated, and some of the women in the bank started looking at me a little differently over the next few days. I didn't care; the poo-poo had hit the fan, and I was just trying to stay out of the line of fire.

About two weeks later, Diana called me and said she would be flying into Amarillo in a few days and wanted to see me again. I got her a room in Dalhart, and we got to know each other a little better. She also got to meet my parents. I told her I would try to take off a day or two and fly to Milwaukee to see her.

I had to fly into Chicago, and Diana picked me up at the airport, and we drove back to Milwaukee. I stayed where the Packers stayed when playing at County Stadium in Milwaukee. I met her folks, and I think Diana's dad wasn't sure what his daughter was doing. Later on, I figured out her dad was narrow-minded about almost everything, not just me.

A few years later, during a visit to Milwaukee, her dad and I drove for six hours to save $2.50 on a radio antenna for his pickup truck.

Things between Diana and I were moving along very nicely, and we started trying to figure out just what we were going to do in the near future. I started looking at bank jobs outside the area, mainly in the Oklahoma City area.

In June, Diana had an offer from the First National Bank in Amarillo, so she moved to an apartment there. I moved in with her, and I drove the eighty-five miles each way to the bank in Stratford. My divorce was final in early June, and the one thing I really needed to do was get the hell out of Stratford for good. The people in the bank were treating me very differently since the divorce. One of the reasons was the man Jeanie was working for had gotten a divorce as well as the couple across the street from where we lived in Stratford.

In September, I was offered a job in of all places Norman, Oklahoma the place where we had met nine months earlier. We moved to Norman and got an apartment and I started to work for the Security National Bank in Norman.

I had been there for about two weeks when I introduced Diana to the President and the Chairman of the Board of the bank. The next day, they both came into my office and asked me if I minded if they offered Diana a job there in the bank. Of course not, I told them, and she went to work in the commercial lending area in the front of the bank. My office was ~~on~~ in the consumer side of the bank. This was working out better than I had ever thought it could.

Diana's divorce was final in September, and we got married on the twenty-fourth of October. We bought a new townhouse, and things were going great in Norman America. The oil boom was really booming by late 1980 and money was flowing like water going over the Niagara Falls.

Okismo was the order of the year in Oklahoma. Okismo is when you drive your new Lincoln from the drilling rig to get into a jet and have dinner in New Orleans just because someone told you the café had good specials on tonight. What was also going on in the banking world in Oklahoma City would take another complete book to describe. Many books have been written about the rise and fall of the oil business in the early 1980s in Texas and Oklahoma.

We started buying expensive cars and selling them to the oilies because if it cost a lot, they wanted to buy two of them every week.

One afternoon, my next-door neighbor asked me if I was a drug dealer. I smiled and asked why he would think that. He said that only drug dealers had four corvettes in his driveway. I told him only three of them were mine and the other one was a friend's car. We got a good laugh and started the barbeque grill. We had a Porsche, three Corvettes, Caddies, and Lincolns, and just about anything else expensive. I bought a DeLorean one Friday and sold it on Monday.

About the same time all this was going on we bought five acres east of Norman and started building a new house. We had met two fellows in the bank in Norman who were from Ghana West Africa. Nee Mensa and Edward Dodo Dempson. Yes, his name was Dodo, but when he arrived in the United States, he learned quickly Dodo was not the name one wanted to be called here in this country. He quickly started using his first name, Edward and was called Ed for short. He was actually Doctor Ed Dempson with a PhD in architecture. Ed did the designing of our country home. It was a little bit different than the average ranch-style tract house. It had an A-frame in the middle of the house and a conventional pitch roof on each side. The plans had a two-car garage off the kitchen. I asked Ed if the A-frame part of the building was cheaper to build. If so, then how big a garage could we build if we did it in the A-frame design. He went back to his office, called me the next day, and said, "Really-really big."

We moved the garage from the kitchen side to the opposite side of the house and built it as an A-frame building. It was thirty feet wide and fifty feet long with three double garage doors and one regular house door. Wow, the darn thing would hold nine cars. This was going to be very good, and we could have a skating rink inside the garage if we wanted one.

The new house was supposed to be finished by the end of September 1982, but things happened, and we didn't get moved into the darned thing until the middle of February 1983.

One day a friend of mine asked me if I wanted a cat, a very unique breed of cat. "Well, if it is not an alley cat, then what is it?"

Well, he said it was a Corvette. I told him, "I never heard of a Corvette Cat." He explained the mother cat crawled into the floorboards of a corvette in his shop and had the kittens. He offered to give two of them to us for our new country estate, explaining they would keep the mice population down. I told him sure go ahead and give me the darned cats. Diana and I named them Pete and Repete, and they were really cute little kittens, black and white. Repete was the male and Pete the female, and they did a lot of things around the country place. Killing just about anything that wasn't bigger than they were. When Pete came of age, she took off looking for some alley cat to get together with, but Repete stayed with us for a really long time. He died just after his seventeenth birthday in 1999.

Ed Dempson and his family became good friends with us, and when they were building our home, Diana brought our friends out to see the progress on the house.

The building crew was in the hole for the septic tank, hooking up the pipes coming from the house.

Ed and his family are from Ghana, Africa, and they speak the Queen's English, along with French and a couple of native languages. The guys in the hole were rednecks from Oklahoma. One of the guys in the hole said just as Ed and his family were getting out of the car, "Hey, look, niggas." About that time, as Ed was coming through the trees, he said, and in the Queen's English, "Oh, I say, my good man, what are those chaps doing in the hole?"

The redneck very quickly looked up at me and said, "Well, I guess I kind of screwed up, didn't I." Yeah, just a little bit. Dr. Dempson is one of the professors at the University of Oklahoma.

Ed called me one day and said, May I ask you a sensitive question?"

"Sure, what you got there, Ed?"

"My son asked me what a nigger was this afternoon, and I told him I would find out the meaning of this word. Is it slang for black people in the south?"

Not knowing exactly how to answer such a question I told him, "Well, yes, it is," and I gave him an explanation of how the word got started here in the US. He understood and just laughed about it.

Roger and Cody were visiting us. I brought the DeLorean sports car home with me that afternoon, and Roger asked me if he could drive it. I told him, "Sure, get in."

We started going north toward the I-40, the road was very hilly, and Roger was not acquainted with this kind of car. We started over a hill, and I told Roger, "There is a stop sign at the bottom of this hill. You might want to slow down just a bit." We were doing about 85 miles per hour when he saw the stop sign and let off quickly while hitting the brakes. Rear-engine sports cars have a bad habit of swapping ends under those conditions. We went through the intersection backward at about fifty miles per hour. The darn car never even got off the pavement and Roger did pretty good keeping the car straight. When it stopped, he jumped out and started for the passenger's side of the car. When I asked him what he was doing, he told me, "I don't guess you'll let me keep driving now."

"Heck, Roger, I think you did just fine, not one tire in the dirt. Get back under the wheel, and let's go."

I think Roger learned I knew he could really drive and I didn't want him to feel bad about the sports car's bad habits.

In the next few months, I bought and sold a lot of cars, and it would have been a lot more profitable if things had not changed drastically in the Oklahoma economy. Penn Square Bank was, as it turned out later, the wildest bank on the planet. When the Feds shut them down it changed everything. I couldn't even hardly give a damned car away, let alone sell one for a profit. I wound up getting rid of all the ones I had and lost about $17,000. I had made very good money buying and selling cars for a few months, but now I was about to lose my ass in the car business.

When Jeanie and I were getting the divorce and were in court, we had already made an agreement between us as to how to divide up the assets. She got the gold mine, and I would get the shaft. She got the house, the car, all the furniture, and just about everything else. I got two suitcases of clothes and a note on the land we sold in New Mexico in 1977. We had agreed this would be fair and no problem. We got in court, and her brother didn't agree and said so to the judge. I asked the judge if I could talk with Jeanie out in the hall and he said, "Okay, just don't take very long about it."

I got into the hallway and told her this interference from her brother was kind of a surprise. We had already agreed on everything but if she let her brother continue, I would ask the judge to have her financial statement brought into the proceedings. She went back into the courtroom and told the judge to disregard the statements made by her brother, and to let the settlement stand as agreed.

I had been receiving a check on this land contract for almost five years with having to call this guy about every six months to get him to pay up. In the spring of 1983, he got three months behind, and I needed the money. I came up with this ingenious plan to get the money, yes, and get it all now.

I sent him a registered letter telling him he was in default on the loan and if he did not catch up in thirty days, I would foreclose on the loan according to the agreements signed. He must have thought I was kidding or something because he didn't do a thing. This was a land contract between two individuals and foreclosing would be very difficult at best. Well, for most people, that's true, but I was clever enough to get the job done.

I was a Vice President in a bank, and I used the power I had to do a little tricky stuff to get the job done. I know the banks don't hire the brightest stars in the sky for all positions. I called the bank that held the title to the land in escrow and told the clerk who I was and did she get the papers of foreclosure I sent to the bank. "Yes," she said, "I have the papers right here. The loan is in default, as stated in the contract, and you have all the necessary papers to verify this. What would you want me to do now?"

"Send me the title to the land along with the necessary paperwork, and we will take care of the rest." She knew I was a vice president in a bank and must know what I was talking about, so she sent me the title to the land I had sold under the land contract. She shouldn't have done this, but she did as directed because I was a "vice president of a bank." Once I had the title in my hand, I called the guy and told him I would have the sheriff's office serve him with an eviction notice within the week. I advised him I was holding the title to the land in my hot little hand. He got an attorney, and they called me the next day. I told him to call me back the next day at my attorney's office, and we would talk.

I was in the attorney's office the next morning and informed them of what had happened in the land deal. They told me what I had done, even though I did everything according to the contract, was not totally legal and could not be enforced in court. Well, that may be true except for one thing: I have the title to the land right here in my hand. I showed it to them, and they couldn't believe how I had obtained it. After I told them how they said that it was very sneaky and asked me what was going to happen now. I told them I thought the son-of-a-gun would get his attorney to file a big lawsuit against me.

The attorney in Farmington, New Mexico, called at the appointed time and said exactly what I thought they would. They filed a lawsuit for $880,000 against me. The attorneys on my end looked horrified, put the other lawyer on hold, and asked me what to do now.

I said, "The land and all they have done to it is worth about $250,000 and they make about $200,000 on the place each year. Suing me for $880,000 is pure crap, let's call their bluff."

My attorneys' faces turned red, and they said it would be taking a really big chance.

"Bull crap, it's a bluff, and we'll call the bluff. Tell them we'll see them in court, and don't give them a chance to say one thing. Just tell them that and hang up the phone."

They did just as they were told, and after they hung up the phone, asked, "Now what?"

"We don't do anything; just see what happens," I explained. I didn't get the words out of my mouth before the phone rang again, and it was the attorney's office in Farmington calling us back. I just looked at my attorneys and smiled. Let's see what the big boys want this time.

The attorney said, "Just what do you want?" We were on speakerphone and they could hear me as well.

I said, "Tell the guy I want to be paid off completely and in not more than ten days from now. I want the check to be hand-delivered to me by courier. When I get the money, I will give the title to the courier in return."

They said it would be done and it was just as they said. I got the money in six days and gave them the title to the land.

What I didn't know until the next day was the fools filed suits against the bank, which held the title in Farmington, and the bank I had a loan with in Dumas, Texas, for which I used the land contract as collateral. Well crap, when these banks called me, I told them it was a bluff and not to worry, I'll take care of it. The lawsuits were dropped against all, but the stupid banker in Texas got so nervous he hired an outside attorney for a retainer of $10,000 to clear up the mess I had got them into. He was pissed about the ten grand, but I told him that was not my fault. I reminded him I had said I would take care of it and he didn't believe me.

"Have I ever lied to you in the past," I asked him.

"No," he said. So, I told him to take the $10,000 out of his Christmas bonus and let this be a lesson for not believing what I have told you. We weren't friends after that, but not a big loss on my part.

I paid the loss on the car business and had some money left over to put in the bank. I also didn't have to put up with calling those jerks for their payments, either.

I had gone to work for Grant Square Bank in Oklahoma City when the car business went into the crapper because the oil business died in the summer of 1982. This bank had no oil loans to speak of, so the bottom falling out of the oil business didn't affect it very much.

Diana was still working for the bank in Norman, and I was with a bank in Oklahoma City, so life was going just fine. During the times of doing the car thing, I made some very wild deals. I went by one car lot on a day the owner was gone, and his wife was running things; well, sort of, anyway. They had some trade-ins in the back they were not going to put out front for sale. I told this gal what I thought they were worth, and she sold them to me right then and there. A 1978 Oldsmobile Cutlass with a transmission problem, a 1976 Trans Am that looked like hell and a Plymouth coupe with some damage to the right front fender. I gave her $3,000 for all three cars just to do them a favor and get this junk off their lot.

I put five quarts of oil in the tranny of the Olds Cutlass, and it would spin the back tires. I washed the Trans AM and sold it for $5,000 in one day. I paid $400 to fix the fender and sold the Plymouth for $1700. The Olds we took to a car auction, and it brought $1000. All in a week's work playing cars.

One day, a customer in the bank said he needed to sell his girlfriend's car because they were getting married, and he was going to highway patrol school. I told him I would look at the car and it was an almost new Camaro with low miles and very clean. I offered him the price from the blue book trade-in value, and they took the offer.

I sold the car in a few days for $2500 more than I gave him for the car and got a 1974 Camaro in trade. The old Camaro would barely run, but it was red and, with a little water, could look decent. We put three cans of STP in the engine, washed the car, and took it to the car auction. It followed another red Camaro that did not sell at $2,300. When our car went onto the floor, and the bid got to $1,000, I told the auctioneer, "It is a sold car." The bidding stopped at $1,155. We were in the back of the auction house laughing about the price given for that sled when a very nice three-quarter ton Ford 4x4 with a new ten-foot overhead camper was stalling out at $2,300. I bid $2,350 and bought it. I took the camper off and sold it for $800 cash and then sold the truck for $4,500 cash the next day.

If the darn oil business had not gone into the crapper, the car game would have been very profitable and somewhat fun.

Well, the oilies were in the toilet, and the car business followed. I made some money and lost some money. I went back to being a banker.

That has been the story of my life: take two steps forward and one step backwards. The only problem is time goes on and you just get older. And there comes the time when you get old enough to not get into crap like that. In my life at now the ripe old age of 64 I'm still getting into more than most people could imagine.

The bank in Oklahoma City was owned by a guy who told me when he got to the City, he had $20 in his pocket and GMAC on his ass trying to repo his car. He went to work for a car dealer as a salesman and, in two years, owned the car dealership. He then bought into a bank and, in fifteen years, owned four banks and had a net worth of about seventeen or eighteen million dollars.

In 1983, he was struck down with a really bad case of the stupids. He thought making money the old-fashioned way was becoming too slow, so he faked some financial statements and got a broker to let him buy eighteen million dollars worth of Washington State Power Plant # 3 bonds. As a banker he could not by law invest more than ten percent of his worth or the worth of the banks in one account. He put it all into whoops bonds, as they were called. In three months, they were worth about seven cents on the dollar. The poo-poo was about to hit the fan. No one ever found out why the Feds were called to take a look at the books of all four banks at once, but they did.

At the beginning of the fourth day, they threw a fit when they discovered the whoops bonds and the amount he had bought. This is what bankruptcy looks like from the top of the pile. He was going to jail and not for just a short while. The banks were either closed (sold) in the same week or sold after the Feds took them over.

A year earlier he had purchased the Firestone family yacht for a million bucks that cost five million to build. His little thirty-two-year-old wife was having a blast going to the Caribbean with the crew of the ship. I bet the crew of five was having a really good time with her as well. It is just amazing what can be heard from crew members of a yacht when I was the one paying the bills for the darned thing. They said she was a really good piece of work, and I think that was not just a compliment.

About a week went by, and the president of the bank, who I had finally become friends with, called me one morning and said, "Let's do lunch at the club (Country Club).

"Sure, I said," and we headed for the club about 11:30 that morning. Jay started telling me what was going to happen at the bank.

He said, "Get the hell out of here as quick as you can and find another job." I didn't get the chance, and Jay didn't either. They fired him the next day and me the next. Oh well, just another career change or something like it was going to happen again.

I think I felt bad for Jay; he was a really great guy. Just after I started with the bank, I kept seeing a name on the large item report each day with some very large transactions. The guy's name was Harold Jenkins, and the amounts were six figures every day. I asked Jay who this guy was, and he said he would introduce me to him when he came in on Friday. On Friday Jay called me into his office to meet Harold Jenkins.

As I walked into the office, I looked at the guy and could not help but blurt out, "Are you Conway Twitty?"

"Yes," he said as we shook hands, "I am Conway Twitty." He continued, "I grew up here in the Capitol Hill part of Oklahoma City and have known J.D. ever since we were kids." We sat and talked for a while, and I must say he was a really nice guy.

Earlier that month, one of the bank customers, who was the president of an insurance company, asked me if I would like to do a side job for their insurance company. He wanted me to put a financial package together for a project they were doing in Branson, Missouri.

So, Diana and I went to Branson to meet with this junior partner. He was reported to have been Sportsman of the Year some years earlier. We met, and he said his wife was going to fix dinner for all of us that night at his house. When we got there, the electric power was out on that side of town, so we all went to a Chinese Restaurant to eat.

The next afternoon, he took Diana and me fishing on Dogwood Creek, and we caught about eight nice trout for dinner, which was fixed at the lodge. Everything went well and we went back to Norman to do the financial package for the Dogwood project and to try to get the financing for the place.

We called the right people I knew, and in a few weeks, we got a phone call from the president of a San Francisco bank. They told me they had a client who wanted to meet with us at the Park Suites Hotel in Oklahoma City the next Saturday morning at 9:00 AM.

We got to the hotel and were told our party would meet us on the second floor. We took the elevator to the second floor, and when we got off, we were met by two security guards. The guards took us to the suite, where two more guards met us. The man we met there was the bank president I had set up the meeting with. We sat down and talked to him for a few minutes when in walked this girl.

Now, I must say I have met many very good-looking women in my life, but this woman was unbelievable looking. Her name was Carmon Cowen, twenty-nine years old, from Ethiopia. Her net worth was 500 million dollars. There were two presidents of banks in the meeting also. They all looked at the package we had prepared and, after about thirty minutes, told us they would get back to us in a few days.

They got back in touch just like they said, and the young lady took the whole package for forty-two million dollars. The Dogwood Canyon Project was built, and when it was finished, the junior partner we met with bought the whole thing from the Insurance Company. Oh, by the way, the junior partner's name was Johnny Morris of the Bass Pro Shops.

It was January 1984, and Diana got run off from the bank in Norman. Now, neither one of us had a job. Things in Oklahoma City were starting to get bad from the oilies going bust. It was not looking very good. I got a call from a lady I knew and found out there was an opening for someone to run the financial department of a government sub-agency. They were looking for two people to fill the jobs, and we applied for them.

We were hired in April and had to move to Durant, which is in the south-central part of Oklahoma. We put the country house up for sale and rented a little house in Durant, and it was not too bad there. We had a boat, and Lake Texhoma was only about ten miles away. This was a big lake with good fishing and great skiing.

This government agency made commercial loans in combination with private lenders like banks. They also worked with customers on product design and marketing and just about anything they needed. We had engineers to help with the company's products. Part of our contract was to give at least twelve seminars on economic development around the contract area. The first of these speeches made me a little bit nervous because I didn't think of myself as a public speaker. To make matters worse, the Under Secretary of HUD, Charles Moon, was going to be there to help us.

We were at the Holiday Inn in Durant to put on the conference with the help of Mr. Moon. I was in the coffee shop in the morning going over my speech, which was written on three sheets of legal paper. Mr. Moon joined me at the table and while talking, he asked me what I was reading. I told him it was my speech, and he asked if he could read it.

He not only read the speech, but he used it in the meeting that afternoon. Now I was not only nervous but now what was I going to say? Not being slow by any means, when it was my turn to talk, I got very clever. I gave the same speech, only backward, and for each point I made, I said, "Mr. Moon said this, and let me talk about this some more."

When the thing was over, Moon came over to me and said, "Very good job." He told me it was very clever the way I covered what he stole from me in the morning. That was fast thinking on your part. I thanked him, and we became friends after that.

The second speech I thought would be a lot easier for there was no Mr. Moon present and I didn't put the entire speech on paper. I had little cards with notes on them. This was going to be a lot better, I thought, as I was being introduced. Just then, two television cameras rolled in from the back of the room. One of the camera's red lights came on just as I got up to the podium. Why the heck didn't someone tell me this was to be on television? I survived once again, and these speeches improved with practice.

When we moved to Durant, Repete, the cat, didn't want to move and took off as we were loading up our stuff. About three months went by. On the weekends, when we were back at the country house in Norman, Diana would look for him, but we never saw him. One weekend, while back in Norman, I was in the upstairs bathroom and heard Diana yelling at something. I went down to see what all the commotion was about, and there was the darned cat. Diana said he was coming down the driveway and saw her and here he came running. After that, the cat never strayed very far from her. Repete became Diana's cat for the next sixteen years.

We continued making loans and starting up new businesses in the area, and the speeches were also getting better. The news media started covering them, from radio stations to newspapers and television. I was becoming somewhat well-known in Eastern Oklahoma.

We got a call from the Congressman's office in Washington one day and I was asked if I could write a speech for a Senator from Pennsylvania by the name of Lowell Weicker. We told them we sure could write this for him and asked when they wanted it. They told us they wanted us to come to Washington, DC, and write it for the Senator. Now, this was going to be very nice to get to go to Washington just to write a speech.

Diana and I got to Washington and found our way to the Congressman's office across the street from the US Capitol. The Congressman called the Senator's office, and they wanted me to tell them on the phone the speech, and they would record it. Well, as it turned out, the speech I wrote was given to a joint session of Congress, and I received a congressional commendation signed by the President of the United States.

We rented the Kerr Center in Poteau, Oklahoma, for one of the conferences, and what a place it was. The house was built by Senator Robert S. Kerr, who was one-half of Kerr McGee Oil Company. Senator Kerr was a very wealthy oilman who got elected to the United States Senate in the 1960's. His estate gave the home to Oklahoma State University, and they rented it out as a hotel and conference center (seventeen bedrooms).

We were there and had a large group of people attend the economic development conference. In this group were about thirty of the most powerful Republicans in the state. I knew some of them, but not all. At the end of my speech, I was answering questions when one of the thirty Republicans came over and said they would like to talk to me when I had a few minutes.

I went over to the huddle of the thirty or so Republicans, and their spokesman said, "We would like to ask you a few questions about your speech." They started by wanting to know if I meant all I had said, and I told them yes. I stated these were not the statements from the department I worked for or the sponsoring Congressman. They were made because this is what I think Oklahoma must do to progress in economic development. It was a little broader than that, it was also what Oklahoma needs to be a better state.

This was the wrong thing to say to these guys, as I was about to find out. The spokesman for the group, a Senator from McAllister, spoke up and, without any warning, said, "We would like to talk to you about running for Governor of the great state of Oklahoma." I didn't know what to say. I was totally dumbstruck. That was one hell of a shock, and I just stood there for a moment, not knowing what to do or say. The Senator went on to say they had been watching me very closely for months and were very impressed with all I had been saying. They saw how much the news media had been following my speeches. They told me the Republican Party would get behind me with money to get me elected as the next Governor of Oklahoma. Well, this was getting serious; what was I going to do now?

I did the only thing I could do. I thanked them very much for their confidence in me, but I felt I must turn them down. I don't want to run for anything, I told them. I could see some disappointment, but I went on to explain there were other men in the State who could serve the state much better than I could. I was very diplomatic about this and was sort of proud of being asked anyway.

We went on with our lending activities and economic development speeches in the State, and things were looking up when the house in Norman sold. With the demise of the oil business, real estate prices had fallen drastically in the Oklahoma City area and we were very lucky to get out of the house without losing any money. With that house off our shoulders, we rented a much nicer home in Durant and planned to stay there for the foreseeable future.

A man from north of Kansas City had a prototype boat and came to see us at Rural Enterprises one day. We looked at the most unusual boat I had ever seen. It was twenty-five feet long and had a tunnel hull with an outboard engine eight feet from the bow or front of the boat. This was the wildest-looking boat I had ever seen. We asked about the performance of the boat and were told it was spectacular in performance and would do many things most boats could not even dream of doing.

We needed to see this thing in the water and took it to Lake Texhoma that afternoon for a test run. Spectacular was a gross understatement. This boat, being as large as it was, would do forty-five miles per hour with a ninety-horsepower engine, and we had fifteen people on the boat. Most boats of that size would not even hold fifteen people and no way run forty-five miles per hour loaded like that. He told us we could put another ten on board, and it would perform the same way.

Wow, this boat was very impressive, and we started talking to them about how Rural Enterprises could be of assistance.

The more we talked, the more interesting the possibilities for this boat company became. A man from Kansas City owned the company, and the fellow who brought it to Oklahoma was a junior partner in the firm. We went to the factory and looked at all they were doing and all the financials of the company. If all was correct, they could have a good thing going for them. The more we got to know the fellow who came to see us, the more we liked what he was going to do with this boat company.

That's where things got really stupid because he started talking to us about buying out the majority owner and running the boat company ourselves with his help. The majority owner was not interested except to get his investment back. We had the means to acquire the necessary money to buy the company, with the original owner taking a long-term note for the rest of the money, about $250,000. We looked at everything as best as we could and decided to do it. It would be fun to own this business and not just work for someone else.

We did it in July 1986 and went to the factory to start managing the company and building the boats. We didn't quit our jobs yet because we had two weeks' vacation coming, and we rented a room on a weekly basis until we got everything settled and going our way. In the two weeks I started finding out all the financials were not correct as far as the books were concerned. Then we went to the bank the company was using. Being bankers ourselves, we knew what to ask and found out the money didn't match their books either. The damned owners were faking everything just to get us to buy the company, and the owner really didn't care if we found out. The reason was he was a Federal Judge and knew he could beat us in court.

I called some attorney friends, and he was correct: it would cost us far more to try to win than it would be worth. I was about as pissed off as I have ever been. Duped by a smartass

Judge, that, so to speak, was above the law. I think he knew it would be too costly to beat him in court.

Well, back to the drawing board. We had used all the time off we had and then resigned to take advantage of this little adventure in the free enterprise game. The whole thing cost us about 10,000 bucks and two very pissed-off bankers in southern Oklahoma. Those two smartasses needed to get screwed because they thought they were the smartest guys in the land. They were out about $60,000, and when they asked me what I was going to do about their money, I told them to take a flying bite at a wild cat's ass.

We did the next smartest thing we could do, and that was to move a long way from there. We were back in the get-a-job mode again.

⊙⁄◌Chapter Ten◌◟

When we met, Diana had been with the Marine Banks of Milwaukee, Wisconsin for about ten years. She left on very good terms in 1980 when she moved to Texas with me. Diana called someone she knew there, and they wanted her to come back to work for them. I got a job with a Savings and Loan which under the bank deregulation act became a regular bank. They had nineteen branches in southern Wisconsin and I oversaw commercial lending for the south half of the branches. I remember I had nine branches under my half. I had an office in the main bank in Milwaukee and one in Racine, Wisconsin.

Diana went back to work for the Marine Bank as branch manager of the bank at Cudahy, Wisconsin, a suburb of Milwaukee south of downtown.

We rented a tri-level house in Franklin, Wisconsin. Repete the cat liked the area because there were other cats close by. Soon, he was running around and getting into fights with the other cats. The vet bill was more than the damned cat was worth by three or four times, but he was our cat.

The winter set in late that fall, and it started snowing. It seemed like all I did after work was shovel snow. By the end of December, I had piles of this crap on both sides of the driveway four feet high. I didn't really like all this snow. In the Texas panhandle, it snowed, and the wind blew, but in two or three days, it would be gone. Here the crap stayed until mid-March. In Texas, it would get cold but not stay that way each and every day. There would be days all winter in Texas that you wouldn't even need a coat. Not so in Milwaukee; it was below zero most nights, and the days it did get above the freezing mark were few and far between.

Roger, my son, wanted to come stay with us for a while, and I told him, "Sure, come on." He arrived in Milwaukee with a little bit of an attitude which I hadn't seen in him before. We had gotten along well enough until now, but he was out of high school, and I didn't really know how he felt about the divorce from his mother. He got a job working on a radio tower, but he really didn't like the severe cold of the north country and quit after a few days.

One afternoon, when I got home, he was drunk and shot a gun in the house while we were arguing. There was no talking to him in the condition he was in, and the police showed up because of the gunshot. He got arrested and spent the night in jail in Milwaukee. I thought his attitude might change, but it didn't, and he left for Texas in a couple of days. I got the gun charge dropped, so there was no problem with the police.

One night, though, while he was there, we went to a festival in downtown Milwaukee. It was a food festival, and there were many foreign foods to sample, and all had a good time. When we left, the snow was falling, and we had almost a foot of the white crap on the ground already. While driving back to the house, we passed a place called Leon's. They didn't make ice cream, but some stuff the locals really liked, which I couldn't eat. I thought the stuff was awful and not fit for human consumption. Leon's has no dining room, and you must walk up to a window to order. Now, as I said, it was snowing, and about a foot of the white stuff was on the ground. It was ten o'clock at night, and it was darned cold out there. About thirty people were standing in the snow, in line, waiting to order this poor excuse for ice cream. Right then and there I knew I couldn't live in a place with this many crazy folks. We had a good laugh about it, but in the back of my mind, I knew we would not live in Milwaukee for many years.

The snow finally all melted, and they were selling the house we had rented, so we found another place to live in Greenfield. The house was on the old Tuckaway golf course. In fact, our house was where the seventeenth green had been. There was a little pond at the end of our backyard. It looked very nice in the late spring, but as summer came on so did the mosquitoes, millions of the little bastards. I don't really like having to spray myself every time I go outside, and there was another reason not to stay in this part of the country.

The house had a great big basement which I liked, one of the few things about the place I enjoyed. I had an idea of taking a wooden model of a bird called a common loon and making a radio-controlled thing that would float. I worked on this little monster for about a month, and finally, after spending about five hundred dollars on it, I had something that would float, go forward, backward, and turn left and right.

Cody wanted to come and stay for a week or two, and he arrived just about the time I got the monster bird finished. The day after his arrival, we took the loon to the pond and tried it out. Well, to my surprise and Cody's, it worked very well. It would go forward at about the same speed a duck would swim. It turned left and right with the rudder just under his little ass. It had a three-blade propeller, just like a speedboat. All the electronics were crammed into his back, and the antenna came out just under his beak so that it couldn't be seen from any distance. The paint job on the loon was very real looking, and from twenty feet away, the thing looked like a real common loon swimming around in the water. This was great, and we were having fun with my creation. After an hour of testing, we got the bright idea to hook some little plastic boats to his butt and see how that looked. We used a monofilament fishing line and attached five three-inch plastic boats to the loon.

The darn thing looked great swimming around the pond with five little boats following it. From the shore, no one could see the fishing line, and it looked like the little boats were just following the damned loon. This was working out to be more fun than I had originally figured. We took the loon to a big city park in Milwaukee where there were some big ponds. We put the bird into the water and started walking around the pond with the loon just swimming along having a good time. There were ducks on the pond with baby ducks following their mothers. Now, there was a common loon with five little plastic boats following it, swimming along with all the other wildlife. I stopped and sat down next to a very big tree and put the radio controller down in the grass so it could not be seen easily. Some men were fishing just down from where I had sat down, and Cody walked on down the shore to where the men were. Now, here came the ducks, followed by the loon.

The men started looking at the monster with the boats following it and no one could figure out it wasn't real. One of the men said, "What the hell is that? Cody didn't let this opportunity pass and said to the men fishing, "Well, ducks have baby ducks, don't they? Well then, in Wisconsin, don't loons have boats?" These men, at first, couldn't believe what they were seeing, and now, to have this smart-ass kid saying that about the loon was more than they could handle. You see, the common loon is the state bird of Wisconsin. One of the men, staring with his mouth wide open, threw his fishing rod into the lake and stomped off. Two of the other men grabbed their gear and headed off as well. The last fellow just sat there looking at this monster and shaking his head.

We laughed and laughed until we hurt telling Diana about our little adventure at the park. That night, we hatched another plan that turned out to be even more fun. We went to the store and bought a Chuck Norris doll about six inches tall with arms and legs that moved. We built water skis for him and built a wing under the skis. We painted them a light brownish, so they wouldn't be seen clearly in the water. We made a ski rope and painted it black and yellow with ski handles that looked very real. The next afternoon, we tried this contraption out, and the darned thing worked. The wing made the Chuck Norris doll float, and with a few weights glued in the right place, the thing would start to tip over backward if no pressure was put on the front of the doll. Hooked up to the duck (loon) with a fishing line that couldn't be seen worked like a charm. We set the loon in the water and the Chuck Norris doll behind him and then we gave it the gas. Old Chuck straightened right up and started skiing across the pond behind the loon.

Now, this was just too cool for words. I am not an engineer, but I am pretty good at coming up with an idea and then figuring out a way to get it built. The darned thing looked so real from the shore that it was scary. The pond behind the house also had ducks on it. Now, it had a remote-controlled common loon that could pull a water skier. We ran the thing until, finally, the batteries had run down. It was getting late, and the sun was going down, so Cody said he would charge the loon while I went in and got a beer.

Diana and I were in the kitchen when we heard a loud explosion coming from the garage. When I was buying parts for building the loon I had told Diana I could get it built for about one hundred dollars. Five hundred dollars later, we had a remote-control common loon. So, when it came time to buy the battery charger, I got cheap and bought one that didn't charge the type of battery we put into the loon. To make a long story short, the darn thing blew up. Cody hooked up the charger to the leads and set it on the garage floor and as he was walking away, he noticed it was starting to smoke. He grabbed the loon, and before he could get the charger wires unhooked, it blew the darn thing to pieces. Not the entire loon, just the underside where the battery compartment was. He walked into the back door of the house with a pale look and with splinters of wood all in his pants. After getting him calmed down a little, we found

175

that not a single piece of splinter had touched him. We must have pulled a hundred splinters out of the legs of his jeans. After about an hour he had calmed down enough to laugh with us about the whole thing. That night, we rebuilt the bottom end and put a new battery in the loon. The next evening, Cody and I bought another charger that worked.

The weekend was here, and all-day Saturday, we ran the loon pulling Chuckey around the pond on his skies. That Saturday, the weather was very nice, and a lot of people saw the monster on the pond and either laughed or ran away. Three nuns didn't quite know how to take what they were seeing so they made the sign of the cross and took off in almost a dead run.

The following week, Cody went home to Texas, and I would run the loon in the evenings. On Thursday night, the phone rang, and Diana answered it. She told me it was ABC Sports on the phone and they wanted to talk to me. I picked up the phone. The voice on the other end said he was with ABC Sports and they would like to come to my house Saturday morning and film the remote-control common loon. "Sure," I told him, "Come over about nine, and you can get all the film you want."

When I hung up the phone, I told Diana the person calling must have been one of our neighbors playing a trick on us. We laughed and went on about our business, not thinking it was really ABC Sports.

Saturday morning came around and Diana was going over to her parent's house and asked me if I was coming along. I just laughed and told her no, I better stay here in case ABC Sports shows up to film the loon. We laughed, and she headed out to her parent's house in Mukwonago, Wisconsin.

About ten that morning, I was sitting around the house when the doorbell rang. When I opened the door, I couldn't believe my eyes. There was a big semi-truck sitting in front of my house with ABC Sports all the way down the side of the trailer. Behind the truck was a white Lincoln limousine with the guy who did the outdoor show on ABC Sports. He came in, and they started unloading equipment for the next fifteen minutes. They had sound equipment, cameras, and enough wire to go to Chicago.

They started filming in my basement and talking about how the loon was built. Then we went to the pond at the end of my backyard and filmed the loon going around the pond with the ducks and baby ducks. Then I hooked the water skier to the loon and they filmed a few minutes of Chuck Norris scooting over the water behind the wooden bird. They told me this would air after the Monday night baseball game. I thanked them for coming and went on about my business for the rest of the weekend.

We watched the baseball game Monday night, and in the seventh inning, they announced there would be a special ABC Sports short following the game. Sure enough, there I was on TV with the wooden loon and the Chuck Norris doll. We got a good laugh, and I said, "I guess that's my fifteen minutes of national fame with a loon and little Chuck."

Two nights later, I got a phone call at about seven in the evening, and it was the producer of the David Letterman Show in New York City. We would like you to be on the show with your wooden bird that we saw on the sports show. I didn't watch the David Letterman show very much; I watched Johnny Carson some, but not much. What I had watched of David Letterman, he seemed to me like he made fun of the people on his show a little bit more than I really liked. So, I told the producer thank you for the offer, but if this was the Johnny Carson show, I would accept, but I really don't want to be on the Letterman Show. That was not the right thing to say to the producer of a national TV show. He made some reference to my ancestry and hung the phone up in a New York second. I guess

I just blew my chance at the big time on TV. I have been told that I am the only person to turn down David Letterman.

The next week, everywhere I went, someone would ask me if I was the guy they saw on the ABC Sports Show. I can't imagine what my fame would have been if I was on the David Letterman Show.

Out of the limelight and back to being a banker once again was just fine with me. I have often wondered what would have happened if I had done the Letterman show, but I didn't, and I can't change the past. I think I have turned down more chances for fame than most people.

The banking business in Wisconsin was not the same as in Texas or Oklahoma. People in the northern Midwest don't do the same things as the ones in the south. The whole thing I was starting to figure out was that I really was southern to the core and didn't want to change. These people were slow to move and slow to do just about anything. We only talk slowly in the South. I would need to walk backward to keep up with most people in the north. I didn't like the way they wanted to do business up here in the frozen part of the US.

I had a customer who built most of the popcorn wagons that sold popcorn in places like shopping malls or on street corners around the country. These wagons looked like circus wagons, and this guy had a very good business. One year he needed more working capital, so we made him a loan on his business and one of his cars as collateral. He paid the entire loan back except for about $12,000. He came in one day and asked me if he could remove the car from the loan so his wife could trade it off and get a new car. With only a small balance left on the loan, why not? The next morning, the senior vice president of commercial lending came into my office and made a big stink about me giving back collateral on a loan that was not paid in full.

After thinking about the way this was said to me, I made another one of my career decisions. Then this fool, who knew about half of what I knew about lending, wanted to come back and, this time, get smart with me. Not a good idea for a boy who has never really worked a day in his life except in an office. I told him off and said if he was in my office for more than five more seconds, someone would need to call for an ambulance to take this piece of crap away. As he walked out, I also said I am resigning as of now. I quickly wrote a letter stating the same and took it to the president's office. I walked into the office and right past the assistant, only asking, "Is he in there?" I gave the letter to the little squirt and said this is effective as soon as I get my stuff out of my office.

That afternoon, when my wife came home, I told her I was done with the banking business and would start looking for something different tomorrow. This shouldn't be difficult because I'm from Liverpool and can do any darn thing. (Read this with an English accent, and it will sound better).

I went to work for a Mercedes-Benz dealer selling cars in Milwaukee the next week. Well, not cars, but Mercedes-Benz, as they told me. They said it would take a little time to get started in this business, and don't worry if I don't sell any cars for a week or two. They didn't know me well enough to say that, and I proved it to them in three days.

The dealership had a used Benz that had been on the lot for more than four months, and the manager told all four salesmen to discount it by $10,000. The third day I was there, I sold the car for the full price on the used car sheet. Then I sold three more cars the next week. At the end of the first month, I was the number one salesman, and that included the manager who could also sell cars. During the next four months, I was the leading salesman for three of them. This was starting to piss off the manager because I was a little unorthodox in the way I sold cars.

One night, just as we were closing, this fellow came in driving a new Rolls Royce. After talking to him for a few minutes I knew he had to be a Mafia boss and from Chicago. We got along great; he told me that not doing things his way has gotten many people messed up. I told him if he didn't buy the damned car, I would call a hitman to shoot his ass. We sat in my office and laughed, and I think I could have become friends with this guy. I think he had never had anyone talk to him that way, and he liked it. I used some Texas slang he never heard before. He did buy the car, and it was the most expensive car the dealership had ever sold. He invited me to come to Chicago and play golf with him anytime I could. I think he and I really hit it off. After he paid for the car, he gave me his business card, which only a few people got. It was his private phone number and the card just said, "We kill Rats." On the straight side of his business, he was in the restaurant game, as he liked to say.

One Saturday morning, the other sales guys had the floor ups and I was sitting in my office reading the paper when a black kid about twenty-two walked in and started looking at the cars. None of the other salesmen would go over and talk to this kid who was wearing a purple jogging suit. After about ten minutes, I walked up to him and introduced myself, and he also told me his name. I asked him what he did for a living and he said he had not worked in five months and then only for five minutes. I then asked him, "Was it a second-round knockout?" He said, "Yes, did you see the fight on TV?" The guy's name was Tyrone Trice, and he was the number one contender for the welterweight belt. I sold him a 300E for his wife's birthday present. The other salesmen got a little mad, but they didn't want to talk to the guy, and so I made the sale.

I could see the manager and the other guys didn't really like me at all. I am smart enough to know when it is time to do something different. I needed to get back to a part of the country where my Texas drawl was understood a little bit.

The part of Texas I came from had winter, but it came and went in a hurry. The doggone winter in Milwaukee comes and stays for a long time, too long a time for a southern boy like me. I started calling Mercedes dealerships around the country and found one in Tucson, Arizona, that needed a salesman with some experience. We flew there, and I got the job in a hurry.

We moved, and I was glad to get out of the frozen north. This was going to be good, and I sure liked the weather. What I didn't count on was that Tucson is about the cheapest damned place on earth. Diana could not find a job that paid anything at all.

Diana was the branch manager of a sixty-million-dollar bank in South Milwaukee, and she could have made about one thousand dollars more per year than she paid her secretary as a branch manager in Tucson. I, on the other hand, did very well selling cars in Tucson for a while.

I sold $175,000 worth of cars the first week I was there. In three months, I was the top salesman at the dealership. In the fifth month, I sold more cars than all the other salesmen put together. In the sixth month, they moved me into the used car department only, and my income dropped by six thousand dollars and the same the next month. The chicken shit manager was listening to the other salesmen complain about me getting all the sales. The month I sold more cars than all the other guys, I didn't even take ups from the floor. I went out to the business people in town and told them I would trade cars with them for a day. Most of the time, they didn't give me the new car back; they just bought it.

One Saturday morning, just as we opened, a woman came in wearing a jogging suit, her hair was in big curlers, and she was wearing very large sunglasses. She asked me if we had a taupe-colored SL Mercedes, and I told her we just got two in, and they were in the back. They had just been unloaded from a truck and were not cleaned up to go up front yet. She said, "Let's go see one," and I took her to the back lot to look at the cars. When we got to the SLs, she said, "Ok, that will do; where do I sign to buy one?" This was a surprise because she said nothing about the price of the car. As we walked back into the showroom to my office, I asked her how she would like to pay for the car. She quickly handed me a visa card and I read the name—it was Linda Ronstadt.

I read her name out loud, and she quickly said, "Don't do that, please."

I just smiled and said, "No one can hear us, for no one is here yet but us." She smiled, and we went into my office to do the paperwork. She sent a guy the next week with a check for the balance due on the car and he picked the car up for her.

The used car department was not going to work well enough to make a living if Diana could not get a good job in this place. It must be time to make another career decision and get the hell out of this place.

We moved to Albuquerque, New Mexico, and Diana got a job very quickly with the Department of Labor for the State. The problem I ran into was that I could not get anything very good because my name was not Jose or something like that it. I wound up selling Hondas and this was not a very good time in New Mexico to be selling anything.

I was not making very much money selling Hondas but at least Diana had a good job, so we were doing fair and surviving in the land of enchantment. I told Diana one day that I should do something different, and she said why don't you go drive a truck for a while? It might make you feel better. I told her I just might and started looking at the trucking companies in Albuquerque. I called a company called Road Express, and they said to come on out and put in an application. I got all the paperwork done, and the manager stated you haven't driven in over ten years. Yes, you're right, I told him, but give me a road test and let's see if I can still drive one of the damned things. He just looked at me for a minute and then said, all right and left his office with me sitting there. He came back in a few minutes with a guy about sixty-five years old and said, "Let's go drive a truck."

He took me to the yard and said, "We will use this truck for the test." He told me to get in and go to the trailer he was pointing to and hook it up. I did which surprised him a little, then he got into the truck. I got in, and we took off down the road. After about thirty minutes, we came back to the truck yard, and he said not one word when he got out of the rig. I followed him to the office where the manager's office was, and the old man went in.

The first words out of his mouth were, "You can send this guy anywhere in the country you want. He has not forgotten one damned thing about driving a truck." He came back out and smiled at me. Then he told me we used a truck with the tach unhooked to make the test very hard, even for a good driver. He kept smiling when he also said, "Man, you can really drive." I thanked him and walked into the manager's office again.

The manager said, "We have some more paperwork to do, but can you take a load to Los Angeles tonight?"

"Sure," I told him, "That's why I'm here."

The trucking company manager shook his head and said, "Well, I guess you're right about that."

I left for Los Angeles that night and was gone for about two weeks on my first trip in a truck in over ten years. It was kind of fun doing it for a while. In fact, so much fun that I drove for about two years on and off.

In those two years, I was in almost every state in the union and in almost all the bigger cities. I went from California to Boston and back many times. On another little trek, I took one from the Mexican border to Canada. After a while, I figured out I was one of the few drivers who never broke anything, and I was always on time. It I might have been a little harder for the company to get along with, but they never said anything because I did the job and did it right.

I picked up a load of grundage in Yuma Arizona that was going to Boston. Oh, by the way grundage is vegetables like lettuce, tomatoes, onions, and the like. Anyway, when I loaded, I was rested and drove all the way to Columbus, Ohio, nonstop except to eat and go potty. Just west of Columbus is a weight and measure station. They are in almost every state, and they check your weight and papers for the load. They also checked the driver's logbook to see if you were only driving ten hours per day. I carried two of the logbooks so I could use one for real and one for faking the number of hours I really drove. I got selected for the complete check over, "the works," at this place when the girl in the window told me to get my logbook and papers, get the log up to date, and come in. There was no way, even with two logs, I could get away with this one. I took the log and load papers into the station and set the log down on her desk. I drew a line where it said driving all the way from left to right straight through. That's driving the whole twenty-four hours straight. Then I said, "You got me," and I stuck out both my arms toward her and said, "Go ahead and cuff me, I'm guilty." She told me most drivers would try to do something stupid with their logbook and would be fined at least $500 for their stupidity. Doing it the way I did, she looked back at me, and I winked at her. She just smiled and handed me the logbook and said go get in your truck and don't move for eight hours and then winked at me. The shift changed in six hours, and I slept for about the same amount of time. I noticed the girl was gone, and some new ones were there, so I hauled ass from that place. I'm not sure I broke a world record, but I got to Boston a day early, and the place where I unloaded the stuff was very happy about it.

The dispatcher sent me to one of the weirdest places in the country to load. It was Saint Albans, Vermont, the land of the little people. I got there in the late afternoon, so I stopped in the first truck stop I came to and slept for a couple of hours. Then I went in, got a shower, and changed into clean clothes. I had dinner, then thought I would unhook from the trailer and look this town over. I couldn't load until the next morning at ten o'clock, so I had time.

As I drove down the main street, I noticed all the people I saw were very short. Like five feet tall or even shorter, so I parked and started walking around looking at the stores on Main Street. I asked the guy in one store about the size of everyone I saw in this town. He told me the town was on the shore of Lake Champlain and that the town was settled by French sailors who were very short. I was having a blast looking down at everyone and saying hello. Being vertically challenged myself, this was great.

I went into a bar, and when my eyes became adjusted to the light, I was sitting next to a guy who was six feet eleven inches tall. He said he was from New York City. He was there to do a job at one of the buildings. Being so tall everyone was staring at him all the time. I asked him if he felt like Gulliver. He just laughed and said, "Yes, I do." We drank a couple of beers, and then I went back to the truck stop for the night.

The next morning, I went to the place where I was to load and it was a chocolate factory called Van Houten and Zoon. I was to load sixteen thousand pounds of chocolate Easter Rabbits for Wal-Mart. This amount of weight would make the trip back across the country nice and easy.

One day, while at home, Diana told me there was a job opening with the Department of Transportation in the State of New Mexico. She had gotten me an application for the job. I had to go take a test and it took almost eight hours to complete. Diana worked for the state so she could get the score from the test, which they didn't give out. They just told you that if you were in the top five, you would get an interview. I not only was number one on the test for that day with fifty-seven people taking it but the highest score in the history of the damned test. I didn't even get an interview. They gave the job to some guy named Jose Gonchous who wasn't even in the top half of those who took the test.

I don't want to hurt anyone's feelings in the land of enchantment, but the place drips with taco sauce, and the ugly factor is high there. They had a king instead of a governor when we moved four years later. This state was stupid enough to elect Bruce King for the third time to that office. When that happened, I knew it was time to get out of Dodge again.

We sat down one evening and talked about what we were going to do. I commented that we should move to Las Vegas, Nevada, and be beach bums. After Diana quit laughing, I told her I was serious about going to Las Vegas to look around. Hell, I told her, your parents have just bought a house there, and they are getting older, and you just might want to be closer to them.

ᑯᔐᓐChapter Eleven ᕞᓐ

I went to Las Vegas in about a week and started looking around at what I might do there. I found a dealers' school on Fremont Street and talked with the manager for a while. It sounded like something I just might do.

I told Diana I could get the government to pay for the dealers' school with a little trickery and why not just do it. Diana's job was on a contract which lasted till the end of the year so on the first of October I started dealers' school in Las Vegas Nevada.

A guy in the school never heard one word being said by anyone for he always had tunes playing through his headphones. The guy never dealt a game in twenty-one weeks of school. The last time I saw him he was at Circus Circus working in the slot department emptying the money out of the slot machines. The only job he was qualified for, I think. All he did in the school was listen to music and talk some about sports betting. Some of the ones I went to school with are still working as dealers, but very few.

On our lunch breaks during the school, we would go to one of the little places on Fremont Street that had very cheap food. One of them had a whole pizza for a dollar. After the school some of us would go to the Horseshoe and eat their $1.99 steak dinner. Price of food was still very cheap in the early nineties. I would eat breakfast at Mary's Diner for a dollar most mornings.

Food in Las Vegas started going up not long after I moved there. Nowadays, the corporations that run most of the casinos want to make a profit on everything from rooms, food and just about anything else.

When the mafia ran Vegas, they gave rooms and cheap food to get the gamblers in the door. Now Las Vegas gets thirty-four million people per year coming through the airport. About another fifteen million people get there by car. When the corporate boys started figuring out they didn't need to have cheap food, the prices went up. And the quality of the food went up with the prices. Vegas now has world-class restaurants with world-class chefs.

The cheap or free rooms are not the normal thing either. Some of the places on the strip are five-star resorts with five-star prices.

When I first got to Vegas, I got a little apartment behind the old Nevada Palace off Fremont Street. At school, I learned to deal Roulette. The next game was craps, and that part of the school took nine weeks to complete.

It was the end of November and I got a job as an instructor for a truck driving school and went to the dealers' school at the same time.

One of the students I was given at the truck driving school was a girl who had never even had a driver's license of any kind from anywhere. She had not ever driven a car and I was going to teach her to drive an eighteen-wheel truck. This was easier than one might think because she had no bad habits to break. Within a week, I had her driving a truck with a set of doubles down a mountain pass that most of the other students were afraid of. She did very well, passed her tests with flying colors, and got a job driving for a big trucking company from Springfield, Mo. Another of my students went to work for Jack B. Kelly Company, who never hired break-in drivers. I taught them not only how to drive but also how to get by on the road. Most of the other schools just tried to teach the students how to shift the gears and herd the things down the road. When I quit this teaching job the management really hated to see me go. I had a job as a dealer and was about to embark on one of the most interesting jobs I have ever had.

Jokers Wild was a new casino owned by the Boyd Group on the edge of Henderson, Nevada. It is a small locals place that had about ten table games, lots of slots, and a cheap buffet. I only lasted thirty days. Companies always hired too many people for the opening and I was one of the people let go when the business slowed to a normal pace after the opening. But now I had some experience as a dealer and was gaining confidence dealing blackjack. It would now be very easy to get another job in one of the smaller casinos downtown.

I got hired at the Golden Gate Casino, which is the oldest casino on Fremont Street, downtown Las Vegas. I improved very quickly as a blackjack dealer there. After a couple of weeks with no pressure dealing, most people thought I must have been doing this for years. I could do something many of the dealers never learned to do. I could talk and deal cards at the same time and not make any mistakes. That is harder than it looks.

I should have stayed at the Golden Gate longer than one and a half months. As I walked down the street one evening after getting off work, I passed by the Pioneer Casino. I went in and asked the pit boss if they needed any dealers, and he gave me an audition right then and there. After dealing a few hands, he took me off the game and asked me when I could start. I told him I could start that evening. So, I gave up the day shift for swing shift, all for an extra $5.00 a day. I still had a lot to learn in my early days as a card dealer.

I worked there for only a few weeks and saw an ad for dealers at the Lady Luck Casino. I applied and got hired on the graveyard shift. That shift starts at 2:00 am and ends at 10:00 in the morning. If the time of day doesn't kill you, the boredom would. We spent most of the shift putting the used cards in order and back into the boxes they came in. At about eight in the morning, we would start to get a few players until the shift was over at ten.

This was going to kill me if I stayed on that shift and I had to find a way to get on a different shift. One day the shift manager from day shift said he was looking to buy an exercise machine for himself and his wife. I said I had one, and it was a very nice one that I wanted to sell. He looked at it and asked, "How much do you want for the exercise machine."

Here was my chance. I told him, "I want $750.00 cash or $250.00 cash and a day shift job."

The next day, I was off then I started on the day shift from ten to six in the evening. Great, this was exactly what I wanted. Nice shift and more money by double than the first dealing jobs paid. Yes, I was going to be a dealer in Vegas, and I was going to like it.

The Lady Luck Casino manager was a woman. She had been the secretary to the General Manager and became a shift manager for two weeks and then casino manager. That's really moving up the ladder in a hurry, but this is Vegas and things like that happen in Vegas. I'm sure it happens everywhere, but I think Vegas does things a little differently than most places. The name we gave the casino manager was the Anorexic Bitch. She didn't have enough brains to get a headache.

The day before New Year's Eve, she fired the entire craps crew on day shift and swing shift. New Year's Eve is the busiest day of the whole year, and we had no craps dealers in the joint. They were running around to all the schools trying to find enough craps dealers to work New Year's Eve. On January third, we had a new casino manager.

I had started at the Lady Luck on the graveyard shift and hated every minute of it. After getting on the day shift, I began to like being a card dealer. I liked meeting people from all over the world, and I enjoyed watching all the people that came through the casino.

I had a fellow at a blackjack table from New Zealand. He had about $2,500 in chips and said that in thirty minutes, he was going to go have dinner. Another fellow sat down and bought in for one hundred and started playing. The guy from New Zealand asked the guy who had just sat down if he was really a gambler. The guy said well, sort of, I guess. The fellow from New Zealand said I am going to go have dinner, and if you are a gambler, I will flip a coin, and the winner gets both stacks of chips, your ninety dollars against my 2,500 dollars. The second guy said for twenty-five to one odds, sure, I will do this. So, I flipped a half dollar with the pit boss's ok, and the fellow from New Zealand won the toss. Another one hundred buy-in, and the man from down under asked, "Want to do it again?" To make a long story shorter the New Zealander won again and left the table. He told me he really was a gambler, and he could tell the other guy was just a loser.

About a year later, I was walking through another casino downtown and heard a dealer telling the same story to his players at the table. One of the players said, "No way did that really happen." I stopped and said, "Oh yes, it really did happen because I am the dealer who flipped the coin."

I am sure there are a million stories about things like that in Las Vegas. There is a new country song playing on the radio lately that says it quite well. God is Great, Beer is Good, and People are Crazy.

I worked at the Lady Luck for thirteen months, and during the last few months, we got these awful, ugly shirts to wear. They were red and yellow and were made from a material that felt like rubber. When I left the Lady Luck for a job at the new Boulder Station, they wanted to know why I was quitting. They wanted three reasons why I wanted to leave, so I put ugly shirts, not enough money and ugly shirts.

One of the floor supervisors at the Lady Luck had gone to work for the new Boulder Station when it opened, and he was a good guy. I stopped in to say hello and look at the new place after it had been open for about a month. He told me they were hiring new dealers and that I should apply. After he told me what the dealers were making at Boulder Station, I decided to fill out an application. I went in for the audition at ten in the morning, dealt a couple of hands of blackjack, and went to the roulette table to audition.

As I stepped up to the roulette table, I noticed one very strange thing. The wheel was on the left end of the table, which made it a left-hand table. It was the first left-hand table I had ever been up close to. The shift manager asked me if I could deal a left-hand table. No problem, I told him and spun the ball like I had been doing it for years. To this day, I'm not sure how I did it.

There were no players on roulette, so the shift manager played, and I dealt only one spin to him . He put up a stupid bet, and after I marked the winning number, he moved it to where he had another wild bet and said, "What does it pay?"

I pulled 112 chips from the rack, pushed them with one hand over to him, and said, "112, sir." He looked at the way I did the payoff and said to me, "Can you start tomorrow night at seven?" I told him I sure could and thanked him, and now I worked for the Boulder Station Casino.

I was put on a left-hand roulette table the first night I worked at Boulder Station, and I had a hell of a time spinning the ball with my left hand. I spun the ball off the wheel into a woman's blouse and into the coin holder of a slot machine. I ended up dealing mostly blackjack after that night.

I became a good blackjack dealer while I worked at Boulder Station Casino. Most of the players were locals, ~~and~~ the tourists stayed on the strip or downtown. We would get a few tourists, but not many. Boulder Station was one of the first of a new group of casinos that were built for the local people of Las Vegas. This concept has worked well for the Station Group for they now have six more of these scattered around Vegas.

Boulder Station dealers made a lot more money in the first years they were open than they do now. It was the beginning of making decent money in Las Vegas as a dealer. I worked there for about eight months. I might have stayed much longer, but I was on a shift that I really didn't like. I worked from 9:00 PM until 5:00 AM. The shift manager was the son of one of the big management people at Imperial Palace on the strip. He must have gotten the job through what is called "juice." In casinos it is mostly who you know that will get you somewhere, not what you know.

I will talk more about this thing called "juice" later when I finally got some of this juice.

This shift manager at Boulder Station was only one of many who got their jobs with juice. Station Casinos in the early nineties had a lot of management who were not qualified for their jobs, but they made tons of money anyway. Their casinos were mismanaged, and despite that fact, they made money hand over fist. As soon as these dummies did something really stupid, they would fire them and find another bozo to take their place. In 1994 and 1995 most of the casinos in Las Vegas were doing very well.

I worked at Boulder Station for about six months. During that time, the shift manager on our shift was fired for being stupid, among other things. The day shift manager was fired for sexual harassment. I just never felt good working there, so I got a dealing job at a small casino on the strip. The San Remo Casino was across the street from the MGM and was a great place to work except for one small problem, we did not make very much in tips. They were nice people to work with, and I would have stayed there if the money had been better. Texas Station was about to open, and I got hired there as a dealer, so I quit and went to work at the new Texas Station.

What a bummer this was going to be. As I said, Station Casinos did not do a very good job hiring management people. Before the opening, we sat through hours of listening to all the rah-rah bull crap: we don't sweat the money here, and we will do everything just right. All that lasted one day when we opened in July 2006. Within three hours of the 10:00 AM opening, the royal flush hit on one of the poker games with a $20,000 payout. And a royal was hit on another poker game with a $50,000 payout. The small-minded management went nuts. The odds of these big payouts hitting the first day are too much to calculate, but luck being what it is, it happened. If the people running the place had thought about the advertising boom this could have been for them, they could have used it to really get a lot of business. Instead, they panicked and started changing everything in the casino. They changed the shuffle every day for a week. They started firing dealers for no reason.

I was walking to the break room, and the casino manager asked me how things were going. I was silly enough to tell him all I had been seeing every day and how I felt about it. The day shift manager was fired the next day, but his assistant now had it in for me. I think he was a little bit scared of me; and he and one other manager cooked up a little idea to get rid of me. It worked mainly because, at the time, I didn't have enough experience in the casino business to know what they were doing to me. I learned very quickly after that, and I got a lot more of what I called street-smart.

Back in Texas and Oklahoma, where I grew up, having a lot of street-smarts was not necessary to get along in the area. I didn't learn anything about screwing people to get ahead in the world as part of my formative years. I was raised to be honest and treat everybody with a certain amount of respect. Hell, I was damn near fifty years old, and I still thought most people were honest and wanted to do the right thing most of the time. This time, they were teaching an old dog some new tricks.

I decided to head back downtown to work. I got a job dealing at the Four Queens, and I worked there for two and a half years. When I started at the Four Queens, they were still a table for table in craps and shift for shift in the rest of the pits for sharing in tips. The second day I worked there, I was asked to sit box on a craps table. This was a real experience in how to hustle the customers. The dealers were English and two of them had been casino managers for casinos in Africa. These guys were very good dealers; in fact, they were too good. They did things on the table I had never seen before. They also made eight hundred dollars each that day and it was in the middle of the week.

I was glad to go back to dealing blackjack the next day. The money we made at the Four Queens was better than I had ever made dealing. I also liked the fact that most of the customers were tourists and not locals. It was going to be a good job except for a few minor things all casinos have. The dealers, for the most part, were easy to get along with and the floor supervisors were okay as well. There was one-floor guy who was difficult to work with, but he was so stupid that most of the time, he didn't bother anyone. We called him Picky Nicky, and that was a fairly good description of his personality.

Nick said to me one day as I was going on break, "That was not very professional the way you dealt three-card poker the last few minutes." I stopped and took the tips out of my shirt pocket to put them in the toke box. I showed them to Nick and said, "This is $85.00, and I didn't give the house away. The dealer before me gave out a straight flush and got only $25.00 in tips; now, who is the professional dealer?" Nick didn't know what to say as I walked away to the break room.

Nick was about the only problem at the Four Queens. He griped about everything that happened. I asked him one day in the breakroom if his children even spoke to him or liked him. He didn't answer me.

One afternoon, on a slow day in the middle of the week, a fellow sat down at my table that had been dead all day. He bought in for $2,000. He started playing one to three hundred dollars per hand and was winning. I was very pleasant to this guy, but I didn't say anything out of the ordinary to him in the twenty minutes he was at the table. As I was going to walk out of the pit to go on break, Nick stopped me and said he was going to write me up for excessive talking to the player. "Never heard of such a thing," I said. Nick was very nervous about the fellow winning a couple of thousand dollars at the table.

"What did I say that was excessive?" I asked. He couldn't answer me, so I said as I walked out of the pit, "I don't think I want to be written up by you for anything," and walked off. The casino manager was standing at the end of the pit and asked me what was going on with Nick. I told him that Nick couldn't handle the fact that the player was winning and wanted to write me up for nothing. I told him to go to hell and walked off.

The casino manager called Nick and me into his office and wanted to know what was going on. As I was explaining to the casino manager, Nick started to fill out the write-up sheet. I looked over at Nick and said to him, "If your pen touches that paper again while I'm talking to the casino manager, I will break your damned arm." The casino manager told me that I couldn't talk like that to a floor supervisor. I stopped and looked at the casino manager and said, "You must be as big an idiot as Nick. If I hear another word of this crap, I will get up and stomp the shit out of you both; now shut up, and I quit," and walked out of his office.

I went straight to the Golden Nugget and filled out an application for a job as a dealer. I was told they would be hiring a lot of new dealers because of the opening of the new Wynn casino on the strip. "Good," I said, and "I would like a month off."

I started at the Golden Nugget the day after Labor Day and stayed there for six and one-half years. The pay at the Nugget was very good, the best for downtown, by far.

Oh, one other thing about the Four Queens: I became the only dealer in the history of gaming to be written up for "brooming a dealer." This will need some explanation. The Four Queens hired a dealer about a year after I started there. Her name was Camille, and I thought she was from Los Angeles, a valley girl by the way she talked. Camille was very good-looking and friendly with almost everyone. About a week or two after she started, I heard one day that she had filed a complaint of sexual harassment against one of the floor supervisors on the swing shift. I heard that the guy just walked by her and she went off on him. *Wow,* I thought, *she sure didn't seem to be that way with anyone on the day shift. She seemed to act fine around everybody on day shift.* I didn't know the floor supervisor on the swing shift. I didn't think too much about it. A couple of days later, in the break room, I asked Camille if she was from Los Angeles.

"Why did you ask me that?" she said, "I am from Tijuana, Mexico," and gave me a go-to-hell look.

"Wow," I said, "You don't have even a hint of a Mexican accent." This was the wrong thing to say to her. She went ballistic and, in a very heavy Mexican accent, said, "Do you think I am a Mexican whore?"

"Sorry," I told her, "I didn't mean anything except you don't have a Mexican accent, that's all." She went wild and started cussing me out in Spanish. I found out later that she went to the casino manager and made a complaint about me for something. The casino manager later told me not to worry about it but just stay very far away from her. No problem, I told him because I thought she was a little crazy.

A couple of days later I was headed back to the pit from the breakroom and passed her in the hallway. She went off on me again and I just kept on walking to the pit and didn't say a word back to her. The casino manager came over to me and asked if I had said anything to her because she had made another complaint about me. I haven't said one word to her and told him about just walking past her going on break and she went off on me again. Three more dealers backed this story up, so the casino manager dropped the whole thing.

I then heard from someone that Camille had been fired from four different casinos for filing complaints against other dealers and floor supervisors for sexual harassment. I was sitting in the breakroom when I heard all of this about Camille, and so I decided to give the little witch a present.

I saw one of the little brooms that the cleaning staff uses to sweep up in the casinos, and I put the little broom handle in the lock on her locker. I said, "If she indeed was going to be a witch, I think she deserves to drive a little sports car." Everyone laughed except Camille. She went straight to the casino manager and filed another complaint. The casino manager must have been just looking at the girl and not what was going on, so he wrote me up for "Brooming," a dealer. When I was in his office and he showed me the write-up, he told me he would throw it in the trash. "No, you don't," I said. "I want to sign it and take it home and frame the thing. It will make one hell of a story to tell when anyone asks about this."

We both laughed, and I signed the damned thing and took it home. Well in the next couple of days, management started hearing about all the things this girl had done in the other places she had worked. You see, in Las Vegas, the community of casino workers talk to each other like brothers and sisters. The casino manager started asking questions at the other places Camille had worked and found out what he had hired. She was fired within a day or two, and no one ever saw her again. As it turned out she had been fired from at least four casinos for doing the same things she was doing at the Four Queens.

I started at the Golden Nugget sitting box in the craps pit. That is the person who sits in the middle of the table and watches the game, makes changes, and a few other things that I won't go into. The second day I worked there, the shift manager, who was a woman, came over to me as I was going to the table. She asked me if what I had on was the only thing I had to wear. Well, I was in banking for several years, I explained, and when I came to Vegas, I only kept the really good suits. So yes, I guess it is the only thing I have to wear. The shift manager then said, "You are making everybody else look bad."

I just smiled and sat down at the craps table, and went to work.

At the end of the first week, the pit boss came over to me and said, "There is some talk about how much experience you have dealing craps." I told him that I had told the casino manager exactly what my craps dealing experience was and asked, "What is the real problem? Was I not doing the job right, or did one of your friends want the job? If so, just put me in blackjack dealing cards, for I really don't like it in craps anyway."

The next week, I was a blackjack dealer and happy about it. Sitting box is very boring and makes the day go by very slowly.

On my first day as a dealer, I was put on a double deck game in pit two. About an hour before the shift was over, the floor man said I was not doing the proper shuffle. I said, "I don't know the right one, but if you will be so kind as to tell me, I will start doing it the right way."

He said, "Didn't you read the book?"

I told him I came from the craps pit, and "No, I didn't read the book." I think he was impressed with the way I could deal the game but didn't want to say anything. I would find out much later what he thought and why.

I worked for about two months, and one day, the shift manager from swing shift came over to me. He told me they were going to need another floor supervisor, and he wanted to ask me if I wanted the job. He explained he had told the casino manager that he thought I would be the best one for the job. I told him thank you and wondered why the swing shift manager would recommend someone from another shift.

The next day our shift manager asked me if I wanted the job as a Floor Supervisor. I told her I did and asked when I would start. She said it would be a couple of weeks. "Fine," I told her, "Just let me know." Five weeks later, I saw the casino manager and asked about the floor job. He told me in some choice words that I would never be a floor supervisor as long as he was a casino manager. I started laughing and told him that was just fine with me.

I learned later, much later, that the deal with the craps pit pissed him off, and I was on his shit list. Riche Mofit was, and I guess still is, one of the biggest horses' asses in the business. He didn't stay long at the Nugget; he went to Treasure Island, and we were all glad to be rid of him.

The new casino manager was a woman who came from the Sands. She was very good-looking and looked nothing like a casino manager. She had big juice with someone high up and got about anything she wanted. She, as the story went, moved up in the company very fast. Sex and very good looks will get you more places in this world than education and brains. The casino business isn't rocket science, and this is Sin City, so that works very well.

She wasn't as bad as the casino manager because she tried hard and did a pretty good job. She was fair to everybody and did not let anything bother her.

The Golden Nugget was bought out, along with all of Wynn's casinos, by MGM. Steve Wynn screwed up a lot of ways and got taken over by MGM about a year and a half after I started at the Nugget.

Nothing changed with the new ownership, except who signed our paychecks, and we were all glad to see this. Some people were a little worried, but it was all the same. The MGM didn't want to mess with a casino that made the money the Nugget did. The casino manager and her hot little body were promoted to casino manager of the MGM, and we got Tom Tewman. Not a good trade. Tewman was a nothing, but someone liked him, and that's how it works in Vegas.

I decided to just lay low and deal cards. I kind of liked the Nugget, and it wasn't a bad job. I was on the day shift with Sunday and Monday off, and the pay was better than average in Vegas. Working for MGM, one of the largest casino operators in the business, had some good advantages. The benefits and vacation time were better than most, and the money was going up every year, so this was where I was going to stay.

One day a rumor started going around in the dealers' breakroom that MGM had sold the Golden Nugget to two guys who had made a fortune in the internet business. Well, crap, what was this going to do to my good deal?

You see, old Steve Wynn wanted to buy the Golden Nugget back, as we heard it, and Kirk, the main owner of MGM, wouldn't sell it to him. As we heard it, Kirk sold the Nugget at about fifty million less to Tim and Tom. These two guys were in their thirties and had made eight or nine hundred million in an internet travel company. They wanted to buy a casino, and they wound up with the Golden Nugget. They came in and had a meeting with all the employees. They told us how great they were and that they were really going to do things at the Nugget. Great, I thought. But they left Tom Tewman as casino manager, and I knew they were really just full of shit.

A year later, they were turned down for a gaming license and sold the Nugget to a guy in the seafood business. In the meantime, Wynn Resorts was going to open and since my wife was executive assistant to the former Governor who was on Wynn's board of Directors, I got a job dealing cards there.

While I was at the Golden Nugget for six and a half years total, my two sons moved from Texas to Las Vegas. There was more opportunity for them in the line of work they did, so they decided to live here in Vegas. This was going to be very good for them to live close to their old dad, I thought. Well, in the beginning, it was great, and we had lots of good times for about a year.

We built a sand rail together. Roger, my oldest son, and I bought a 1984 Olds and cut it down into what later would be a very cool sand car. We moved the engine back three feet and then built, with my youngest son's help, the entire car by hand. We started in March and finished it in late August of 2003. I spent about $14,000 on the sand rail when we, or I, got it the way I wanted it to be. The boys didn't have the money to spend on this project, but I told them that I would pay for it all myself. These two guys are very talented and can build just about anything. That might sound like I am bragging about them and I am because it is true. Later in this writing I will tell just how good they are when it comes to cars and things like that.

We put an old Sprint car engine in the rail car, hand-built all the roll bars, and fabricated the entire front-to-back car from bumper to bumper. We painted the rail a very bright red and put huge sand tires on it. It was one cool rod and also ran fairly well. The engine ran well until I pushed it a little bit too hard at Dumont Dunes, California, one Sunday in the late spring. The engine was just a 305 CID, and when I climbed the comp hill at Dumont, it damaged the motor a little bit too much. Nothing a lot of money can't fix. The car sat in my garage the rest of the year, doing nothing.

Early that year, both of my sons moved back to Texas. They needed to see the old home country again and try making a living there. After about a year there, they moved back to Vegas. We had a disagreement when they left, and I had not talked to them in a year. One day in March 2004, I was standing in my garage talking on the phone, and this new black motorcycle pulled up in front of my house. I told whoever I was talking to that it looked like one of my neighbors just got a new bike and wanted me to see it.

I walked to the end of my driveway, and the motorcycle rider took off his helmet, and it was Roger, my oldest son. He told me he had moved back to Las Vegas and told me he was sorry about the problem we had a year ago. To make a long story short, we put our arms around each other, and that was the end of that. About three months later, Cody, my youngest son, also moved back to Vegas.

All the things that caused them to go back to Texas had been forgotten and forgiven, and I was happy they were back here again.

I had blown the engine in the sand car and wanted to make it run again, so I ordered an AR Racing 388-inch Stoker engine, and we put it in the hot rod. I had put a Chancler tranny in the thing while they were gone, and with the new engine, it ran like a scalded dog. It would go anywhere in the dunes and very fast also. We had a great time running the thing. I sold it three years ago and got over half my money back. I have learned a lot of lessons in life, and one of them is that fun costs money.

Wynn Resorts was about to open, and I wanted a little time off. I gave a two-week notice at the Golden Nugget and took my remaining two weeks' vacation in March. Wynn was going to open on the fifth of April, and that would give me some time off, which I thought I really needed.

We went to San Diego, then spent a couple of days in Mexico and had a really great time. We parked our camp trailer at a KOA in Chula Vista. We always stayed at the Chula Vista Marina campgrounds, but that year they were full. Our visits to Mexico proved they were trying to get the same prices as in the USA, and it was killing their business. Five dollars for a margarita and seven dollars to park. We haven't been back to Mexico for five years. I'm sure they can get along without us, but maybe not.

I started at the Wynn Resort in April, and for the first year, it was great. A job dealing cards that paid over $100,000 per year. They offered me a Pit Manager's job, but I said I would rather just be a dealer—for the money.

I was off Sunday and Monday, and on some of the Mondays, I would have lunch with my sons Roger and Cody. ~~On~~ One Monday, the boys called me and wanted to have lunch. When they walked into the café, they were holding a folder, I wondered what they were up to.

We ordered our lunch, and Roger started by setting the folder on the table and saying, "We would like to talk to you about a business plan we have put together to see what you think."

"Sure," I said, "Let's take a look." Roger started by telling me they had been working with cars for a long time, and they had built some pretty wild cars. I agreed and started wondering what they were going to say next. Cody then told me they wanted to build a kit sports car and he would put in one-half the money if I would go in with them and supply the other half. They said they wanted to build a Shelby Cobra. I will admit their plan was fairly complete, with most of the costs for the car. They said they could make a part-time business building cars from FFR. FFR is Factory Five Racing. I had not heard of them, but the boys explained they were the leading maker of the Cobra and the Daytona Coupe kits.

Cody said he could put in twenty-five thousand if I would put in the same amount. They said the car could be finished for about forty to forty-two thousand. They had all the numbers and costs for the car and starting a business that would be called Vegas Venom. I was impressed, to say the least. They had a fairly good plan on paper, and it was evident they had spent a lot of time putting this all together.

Diana and I talked this over with the boys and agreed to help them with this project. I had seen the Shelby Cobra when they came out in September of 1964, and it was the coolest car in the world. Now, over forty years later, the Cobra is still one of the most sought-after sports cars in the world. Little did I know how much money this was going to cost me. We ordered the Cobra kit in March, and it came in the first week of June.

Roger and Cody built this first car in five and a half weeks, part-time. Most nights, they worked until midnight and all weekends. By August, we had a blue Cobra with white stripes with a 342R Roush engine. The thing ran so well that it blew my mind. This engine put out 450 horsepower and the car only weighed 2,150 lbs. The car was a little hard to drive because we put on tires that couldn't handle that kind of horsepower.

I remember back in September 1964, I was working in Oklahoma City and saw my first 427 Cobra. I was going down 23rd Street when I saw the car coming up behind me. I didn't know what kind of car it was. It was British racing green with big side pipes, and it looked somewhat like an MG. The thing pulled up beside me at a stoplight, and it had a 427 Cobra on the side of the car in front of the door. I had no idea what this thing was, but it had a Richardson Ford plate on the back, so we went there that evening to look at one of these things.

We got to the Ford dealership and went in. There in the middle of the showroom was this little two-seat roadster with a 427 Ford engine, and the salesman told me it was a Shelby Cobra. From that day on, I wanted to own one of these wild little sports cars. I saw a lot of the races where this little car ran off and left everything on the racetracks. Now, I was going to have one of these little monsters. And a monster it turned out to be. With over 450 horsepower and 2,150 pounds, it was a hand full to drive.

In August, the second year of Wynn Resorts opening, Wynn announced it was going to open Wynn Macau in China. Doing some research, I found out that Macau was about thirty-seven miles south of Hong Kong. I called my uncle and talked with him about China and especially Hong Kong. He knew Macau and definitely knew Hong Kong, as he had been there more times than he could count for Phillips Petroleum. When I asked him if I should consider going, he told me definitely yes. It would be an experience and one that I wouldn't have even thought about doing on my own. So, Dave Hennings and I talked about going for the first month to help with the opening. They needed ninety people to apply to spend a month in China. Dave and I signed the slip and received a letter of thanks, but no thanks. Tom Tewman was the casino manager and did not like Dave or me. Diana, my sweet wife, was the executive assistant to Nevada's former Governor. The Governor was also on Wynn's board of directors. One thing the casino manager didn't count on when he turned us down was the Governor knew we wanted to go to China. To make a long story short, we got a second letter from the casino manager congratulating us on being a part of the team going to China to open the new Casino.

The week before we left for Macau, there was a meeting for all the dealers at Wynn Resorts in Las Vegas. Steve Wynn shocked the hell out of us by saying he was going to take about twenty percent of the dealer's tips and give it to the Floor Supervisors. They were getting about $65,000 per year, and Steve said he wanted to even out the pay with the dealers. There is still a lawsuit filed by the casino dealers pending in court to get their full pay. All of this started with the family of a casino player who had lost about four hundred thousand dollars. At first, he was winning big and getting very drunk in the process. While he was winning the big money, he set a world record for tipping. He gave a cocktail girl over two hundred thousand dollars. This is no bull crap, it was over $200,000 and tipped the dealers over four hundred thousand dollars. Then he started losing big time. His family sued Wynn. This pissed off Steve so much that he came up with this little plan to rip off the dealers who he blamed for the suit.

I'm not the judge in this case and I have no idea how it will all turn out, but the stealing of dealer tips by Steve Wynn or any boss anywhere should not be allowed. No one did anything wrong and Steve Wynn just did what he has done many times in the past—he let his emotions control his actions. He would have gone down in history as one of the great innovators of Las Vegas. If he loses this suit, he will go down in history as just a thief.

With this type of news, we were glad to be leaving town for a while, with hopes things would settle down or Steve would see the error of his ways. So, we packed and got ready for our journey to China.

Our spouses went with us for the first eight days of the trip to Macau. They had checked out separate flights and with the hotel rooms being covered by Wynn, they decided to join us on this little adventure.

Now, Macau is an island, so to speak. The land area is approximately twenty-and-one-half miles, and it has had over 650,000 people. And during all the preplanning meetings for this excursion, we were told and given cheat-sheets to translate their Cantonese language to English. As soon as we got off the planes at the Macau International Airport, we found out the predominant language was actually Mandarin or Portuguese. Now, this was going to be fun. Very few people spoke English, so our challenges were only beginning.

After checking into the hotels, Dave and Mila at the Landmark and Diana and I at the Holiday Inn just down the street started exploring this place. With so many people in such a small space, the mode of transportation was mopeds, thousands of them. There were parking lots dedicated to them and lots of street parking as well. Not many cars to be seen anywhere.

And we found out that Macau had its own money—Pataca. Hong Kong and Mainland China used the Hong Kong dollar. And neither really liked using the other's currency. We made numerous trips to the cash exchanges to change American dollars to Patacas, and then changing Patacas to Hong Kong dollars based on our travels for the day.

The language was an issue, and so were the eating places outside of the hotels. Thank goodness it was a former Portuguese colony, as one restaurant we found was Portuguese, so we could at least read the menu in Spanish. The rest of the restaurants were in the native tongue of this island, and if they didn't have pictures of their menu items, we didn't take the chance to eat there. No telling what they would serve us.

We spent a day in Hong Kong and were completely amazed: pedestrian walkways above the streets and escalators going up a mountain with retail shops on each floor and both sides. And they had a tram going up the side of the mountain that was a bit scary. At the top, we could see forever and towered above all the massive high-rise buildings. And there was a Bubba Gump's restaurant at the top.

Hong Kong was amazing, and the majority of people, including the cab drivers, spoke English—the Queen's English. We hailed a cab and told the driver we wanted to see Hong Kong and especially take a sampan ride. So, he took us to an area that had just that AND an island restaurant. He gave the older Chinese woman instructions about what we wanted to see and where we wanted to eat. She did not speak or understand any English. She took us in her sampan around the Bay Area and then to the island restaurant that would be considered a ten-star in the States. Since the restaurant was in the middle of the bay surrounded by water, the only way to get there was by boat.

The tables had turnstiles in the middle, and when the food was delivered, it was put on the turntable so everyone could share. What a concept. When we were done, we simply hailed a boat and got back to shore, where taxis were waiting to get us back to the port where we would catch the jet boat back to Macau.

We had heard about this huge shopping market in Zhuhai. So, Dave and I decided to get a Visa through Wynn for all four of us to go. When we got off work that day which was just initial orientation, we walked to the border of Macau and Mainland China. After getting through Immigration, which was definitely a chore because the Chinese do not like Americans— period, we walked out of the building to an amazing sight. Concrete slabs led to a set of stairs going down. Once down, we found four to five floors of shopping booths. They sold what are called "knock-offs," items that looked like the original Rolex watches, Canon cameras, and more but weren't. The whole day was spent checking out the shops and dickering about the prices. That was the whole idea when shopping here, arguing with the shop owner or worker about the price. We had an amazing time and found a few bargains we couldn't pass up.

The gals went home the day of the opening of the casino. Dave and I were now staying at the Landmark Hotel just down the street from Wynn's, and we could walk to work in five minutes.

After they left, I caught the crud. They called it the Zhuhai flu. I felt like crap, not sick enough to go to bed, just sick enough for everything to taste like hell, and feeling sick to my stomach all the time.

China was worried about what they called the Bird Flu. I'm not sure if it was really that bad, but they cooked everything to the consistency of a Lay's Potato Chip. The food was horrible, and in the twenty-eight days I was there, I lost seventeen pounds. Yes, that didn't hurt me any to lose the weight. Skinny, I'm not, but staying hungry is something I can't stand either. I finally located a McDonald's and a Kentucky Fried Chicken at the Sands Casino in Macau. They and Pizza Hut kept me from starving to death. Oh, if you are ever in China, you have to go to a Pizza Hut. You won't believe it, but they are a five-star place there.

We got the casino opened, and I was a little shocked at the way the Chinese played. These people like to gamble, but they don't drink booze while they play. They are serious gamblers. They drink milk and tea. They laugh when they lose and get serious when they win, different, to say the least. We didn't have much of a problem with anyone in China. The people were nice enough. We didn't understand them and they sure as hell didn't understand us.

I had an idea of what China might be like before I left Las Vegas, but my idea was nothing compared with what that country really is. I expected it to be somewhat like Mexico, just not quite true. China, or at least the part we saw, was much cleaner and more modern than I would have thought. I didn't go into the outback, so I can't judge the whole country. The Hong Kong area is modern and fairly clean. The air is heavy with moisture and I couldn't see as far as one can around Las Vegas.

The one thing I couldn't get used to was trying to travel outside of Macau. Everywhere you went and when coming back required going through immigration and having a visa – both ways. The travel is so restricted and being from the USA, that was hard to take.

One day, a group of us decided to go to Zhuhai again. So, once again, we applied for a Visa to go there. Now the army in China was very strict about their Visas. If more than one person went, the Visa listed all names. Going through immigration requires a Visa and your Passport. The proper way to enter their country was in the order listed on the Visa. The army would get very upset if they had to look for your name on the Visa. Well, on this particular day, the other folks decided not to go, so that left me alone with the Visa. I did what any red-blooded American boy would do to help the Army out. I crossed out the names of the other people. That did not sit well. The Army head grabbed me, walked me to the wall, and told me to stay there. He had the Visa and my Passport in his hand. After about thirty-five minutes he came back and told me to never, ever mark on a Visa again. According to him, it was HIS Visa, and you ~~had~~ "no mark" on it, he told me in broken English. Then he told me I could go, after I told him I was sorry and wouldn't do that again. Well, there was a little problem – he still had my Passport. I asked for it, and he made me wait a bit longer and then told me to go. I headed into Zhuhai to do some more "knockoff" shopping.

We got back to the good old US of A. After traveling about fourteen hours I almost kissed the ground when we arrived in Los Angeles. It was definitely an experience going to China, but I was so glad to be back home.

I went back to work at Wynn Resorts, but things were different. The deal with the tips was heavy on everyone's mind. There was a lot of grumbling and griping and hate and discontent. I took some time off that fall using the disability insurance I had bought. Little did I know just how glad I was to have that policy?

I stayed in pit three for the next year until we left on vacation. Pit three was games like Three Card Poker, Texas Hold 'Em, and Caribbean Poker. It was a good deal for me, and I would be there now if it were not for the back problem.

I did deal blackjack one more time before we left on vacation. It was toward the end of June, and when I looked at the schedule, I noticed I was to be in pit one on a blackjack table. The shift manager walked over to me and asked if I wanted to deal twenty-one for a day.

"Sure, I don't care, not a problem." He told me I would have a player that is the biggest one in the world. "Wow," I said, "Who?" Whatanobbie, and this name is misspelled on purpose. Otherwise, the spelling and the name would not match. That is how it is pronounced. Well, this cat sat down at the table and started playing $75,000 per hand. Now this is serious gambling, and I kept thinking to myself each time he put up a bet, this kind of money could make my year. I have never had this kind of money, but I sure would like to try it for a couple of months. Well, he kept losing and then finally left the private table which was reserved for him.

ᏟᎦᏡᏟhapter Twelve᏿ᏩᎲ

W e left on vacation on July 6, 2007, headed for June Lake, California. On the way there, I started getting a little pain on the right side of my ass. I thought it might be from tension and maybe from the strain of getting everything ready for this two-week vacation. It was not very serious, and all I could think about was how great it was to finally be going to the mountains for two weeks.

We got the camp set up and started to relax a little. On Monday, we rode the motorcycle up the mountain on Tioga Pass to the entrance of Yosemite National Park. It was a great ride. It was also my sixty-third birthday and I got the senior National Park Pass.

On Friday, we headed to Reno, Nevada, to meet up with my cousin Curtis and his wife, Carolyn. Here is where all the problems started with my back. I could barely walk and was in a lot of pain. The next morning, after attempting to get some coffee in the lobby and hobbling back to the hotel room, I got a quick trip to the ER. The doctors there gave me the bad news about my back. They also encouraged me to quit doing what I was doing, or I would be a cripple for life. With that news spinning in my head, we made it through the weekend. On Sunday, we left, and Diana drove us back to June Lake.

I spent the next three days sitting in a lawn chair, feeding peanuts to the Chipmunks and thinking about what I was going to do. We decided to go back to Las Vegas on Thursday instead of waiting for the weekend.

Once back in Las Vegas, I started talking to the disability insurance company about the problem I was having. I also talked to the people at Wynn Resorts about it. By this time, I had decided I was going to retire completely, and forever. No more work for me, not now, not any time in the foreseeable future.

With the X-rays and the ER report in my hand, I went to my doctor in Las Vegas and talked this over with him. This doctor turned out to be a complete bozo, and in just over a month, I changed doctors. This turned out to be a very smart move for me. This new doctor agreed with me on what I should do to be fully retired and get disability insurance as well as Social Security.

This doctor sent me to a specialist, and within a few weeks, I was on full disability from the insurance company and from Social Security.

The first six months without a job, I spent catching up on little things I had needed to do for a long time. It seemed strange not having to get up and go to work. I often thought, '*When did I have time to work anyway?*' I stayed busy and didn't have much spare time. Then, the reality hit me that I was retired. The next six months weren't nearly as easy. I hadn't planned on retiring at this age. I thought I would be in the casino business for a lot longer. Heck, I really enjoyed it. I didn't like the casino's knee-jerk way of doing business. Thinking back at how I worked my way up from working in a break-in house to being at Wynn Resorts, I knew I would miss dealing to all the fascinating people I had met. I dealt to quite a few famous people, too.

At the Golden Nugget, the Amazing Jonathan, comedian and magician, was in the showroom. I was working the day shift, and he would come into the casino early to prepare for his show. He and I got along quite well when he played blackjack at my table. We talked about a lot of things. One day, when he came in, I was dealing to a full table.

He walked up to my table, and I told the players, "Look, it's the Amazing Jonathan, a funny and good magician."

Jonathan laughed and told the players, "I'm not that good of a magician, but this guy is. He can make a $100 bill disappear, and you'll never see it again." Everyone laughed. I dealt to Steven Spielberg at the Nugget and he was quiet and reserved.

As a dealer, I was also an entertainer. Heck, if the people at my table were here to be entertained, I would do just that. One day, a young man sat down at my table, and after he told me how many chips he wanted, I asked him, "What part of Texas are you from?" His accent was definitely not from the US of A.

He laughed and said, "I'm from Norway." I told him we had just bought some Ekornes chairs, which are made in Norway, and we really liked them.

"Oh, so do my parents in Norway. They watch Jeopardy every night sitting in their chairs," he said.

I asked him what his parents did in Norway, and he said, "They are the King and Queen of the country."

I laughed and said, "That would make you the crown prince of Norway."

"Don't say that too loud," he said. "I don't have any bodyguards with me!" We both laughed and settled into playing cards.

At Wynn, I dealt to Mel Gibson, who was a really nice and friendly guy. Others included George Lucas, Paul and Paul Jr from the Orange County Choppers show, and Antonio Banderas. Now Mr. Banderas, when I looked at him with a knowing look, told me he didn't want any attention. So, I called him Jose Gonchos, and he laughed at that. So, he played at my table for quite some time. There were many others, including famous basketball players, hockey players, and baseball players. They all enjoyed being at my table and, while in Vegas, always looked me up. I wanted everyone to enjoy themselves.

When a new player would come to my table, I always asked them, "What part of Texas are you from?" This generally brought out laughter and an explanation of where they actually were from. I played a game of guessing where people were from as they walked up, so my "hello" line was just to get them relaxed and ready to be entertained. And I was pretty accurate!

As the second year of not working came, I started to relax and enjoy my time. I quit being in a hurry to do anything, and everything started working out much better. If I didn't get it done today, no problem; I just did it when I wanted to.

I am starting to really feel retired now, and it feels great. Play golf, ride my motorcycles, and drive my Cobra. Yes, retirement is going to be what I had always dreamed it would be.

I was taking the Cobra to a lot of car shows and riding my motorcycle a lot. Then there was golf, and I was getting a desire to play again and play better than when I was younger. I bought a practice cage for golf, put it in my yard, and started hitting a lot of golf balls for practice. Roger had a renewed interest in golf after twenty years of not playing. Some of the guys Roger worked with were learning to play, and so we all started getting serious about playing better golf.

The boys started building the second Cobra, and they wanted it to be a much better car than the first one. Hell, the blue Cobra was really nice and with a 342-inch Roush engine had 450 horsepower. The Cobra only weighs 2,150 pounds, so with that much engine, it was a handful to drive.

The little Roush engine was like a hopped-up small-block Chevy engine. The RPM would go from idle to seven thousand in the blink of an eye. We put BF Goodrich TA tires on the blue Cobra, and that was a mistake. The thing was like a skateboard on ice. At one hundred miles per hour, you could go to fourth gear and spin the tires. Going through the gears hard was a real thrill, trying to keep the little Cobra going the way you wanted.

One Friday night, we took the little monster to the drag races they had for streetcars. Each of us took turns driving it, and that was a blast. Roger tried to start in first gear on one of the runs, and when he went into second gear, the Cobra changed lanes. When it was Roger's turn to drive again, the starter told him to go alone because he was too dangerous to have someone else in the other lane with him.

We had a good time that night and also learned a lot. Each of us drove the car twice and ol' dad had the fastest run in the Cobra. I may be getting older, but I've still got it sometimes.

Roger, Cody, and I started going out to the desert and shooting guns a lot more than in the past few years. I had bought a Weatherby 257 mag, three pistols, and a 7mm mag, and we were having a lot of fun shooting these guns. Over the last three years, I have increased the number of guns I own to twenty. We have also bought thousands of rounds of ammunition. With the state of the United States, I think it is better to be prepared than hoping for the best.

In November 2008, we sold the Blue Cobra to a gold miner from Elko, Nevada. We only got the amount of money for the car we had in it. The car had over two thousand miles on it, so I guess it was a good price. The new cobra was finished in August 2009. It took two weekends to paint the car. It had six coats of paint and eight coats of clear coat on it. The cost of the paint was $3,900.00. That does not include the labor. If this paint job were done at a custom paint shop, it would have cost over $15,000, just to paint the car. Roger polished all the sheet aluminum under the hood to the point that it looked like chrome.

The engine in the new Cobra was a Roush 427 with over 550 horsepower. The Cobra only weighed 2,150 pounds, so with this much power, it is one of the fastest street cars anywhere. We also put a very good set of tires on this car so that it would handle the huge amount of power. The new Cobra was black with silver stripes. Roger named the paint color the French word for black, which is "noir." He said it is called North American Mohave Deep Strike Noir.

After three years of being retired, I am getting along just fine. I don't get in a hurry anymore; I don't need to. I tell people I have nowhere to go and all day to get there. I don't think I have been bored yet, just sometimes I do very little. It's nice not to do anything sometimes.

I keep in shape, which I believe is the key to being able to do most things after sixty-five. I don't have much wrong with me except for my back, so I do more than most people my age. I have an inversion table that turns upside down, and I use it every day. I think this has kept my back from getting worse. I exercise a lot and play golf.

The Sunday after Thanksgiving I walked out into the backyard of my house. I was having a smoke and saw out of the corner of my eyes, movement over by a big rock in the yard. I walked over, and there was a rabbit just sitting next to the rock. I reached down and picked up the little guy, and he was not trying to run away or anything. This rabbit was not just a small cottontail. He was, as we found out, a full-blooded Mini-Rex exotic rabbit. He had the wildest markings I have ever seen on a rabbit. He was black and white and on his left side was a perfect "W" and some other neat markings. Well, we put up posters on all the post office boxes, but no one claimed the bunny. We fixed the exercise room with a cat potty box with water and bunny food. Two and a half years later, Mr. Wabbit is still part of the family. He is a hoot.

About a year and a half ago, we started looking at the housing mortgage crisis, which was growing way too fast. Both my sons had bought homes in Vegas when they moved back. Both had $300,000 mortgages, and their homes were losing value so fast that no one could keep up. It is stupid to keep paying on a $300,000 mortgage when the value of the house is now only $100,000. Roger was getting burnt out being a mechanic at a Chevrolet dealership and had been looking into a new job for a couple of years.

Roger was looking into becoming an insurance adjuster for crop insurance in Texas. I told him in the fall of 2009 that at forty-four years old if you don't do this now, you will never do it. Well, he did and now works for the largest crop insurance company in the country and lives in Childress, Texas. He just walked away from his home here in Vegas and moved back to Texas. We looked at the mortgage on his home and saw the paperwork on the mortgage was a mess. We didn't know what to do about it and Roger just gave up and moved. I sure as hell didn't blame him for that.

A short time later, I heard about a process that might have helped him, but it was too late for Roger. I called the people who had developed the process and asked a lot of questions about what they were doing. I got a copy of their paperwork, and after reading it, I knew it would work. Not very many people would have the knowledge or experience to complete the process. I asked how much they wanted me to purchase their product for, with the right to resell it if I modified it. I paid the price and got a copy of a process that, if used correctly, could stop the mortgage companies cold.

Diana and I have worked on modifying the process for a year and a half. We found twelve people who needed help and started working on making this legal process work. I am retired, I thought, until we got into this knock-down, drag-out fight with these chicken shit banks that hold most of the home mortgages in this country. The housing market was crashing, the stock market was crashing, and Congress rejected a bank bailout. The banks and mortgage companies wouldn't try to help people who were buried in their homes, lost their jobs, and just couldn't make payments. All they wanted to do was foreclose. And even foreclose on people who weren't late on payments. The whole situation was totally out of control. The casinos stopped expanding, so the construction industry virtually shut down. And the casinos started laying people off. In most households, both people worked, but if they both lost their jobs or even just one, they couldn't make the full payments owed on a house they could no longer afford. And they couldn't sell it either; they owed way more than the house was worth. And the banks wouldn't work with them to adjust the amount owed to align closer with the value. Many people just packed their things and left for another place where they could get a job. As they drove out of the driveway, the keys to the house would be thrown at the front door.

The people who sold us the package would not even know it in its present form. We changed about everything in it and have five cases in the United States Federal Court and two cases in Nevada District Court. We have learned more than anyone should ever know about how to sue banks. The big banks have become so dishonest in the way they handle the home mortgage business that if I were running things, I would have them all shot on-site. I guess that is one of the reasons they don't let me run things for the country.

Some of the problems we have encountered suing the banks have been very interesting, like getting the federal judges to follow the laws. We learned the hard way when most of the cases have been dismissed. The big banks had legal teams readily accessible, and the judges didn't like someone coming into their courtroom without an attorney. Oh, and they got a lot of financial support from the big banks when they were running for re-election.

We are still fighting with the bank over our house. We have been at a stalemate for over two years now, in the summer of 2013.

At the beginning of 2012, we started talking about getting out of Las Vegas. Diana had retired and wanted to go back to Green Country. She was getting tired of the desert atmosphere and the unrelenting heat.

In May, we packed our new camper, a thirty-five-foot toy hauler, and headed for Texas. We stopped in Amarillo for a few days to visit with Roger. He had transferred to Amarillo during the spring and bought a house on the south edge of Amarillo, just west of the interstate highway going to Canyon, Texas. The first few days, the wind blew 30 to 40 miles per hour. We couldn't live here again. We headed for Weatherford, Texas, and stayed in a very nice campground west of town for ten days, looking around the area for land to buy. They are very proud of their land in the area. I guess too many retiring business people were buying land and building show places to prove how successful they have been.

We decided to go to Eastern Oklahoma to look around. We worked in the area in the mid-80s and liked some of the areas. We found a KOA in Sallisaw which we thought would be a central location to look around from. We found a nice real estate lady to show us around and, in the first few days, looked at four or five places in the area.

The first Saturday we were there I told Diana that one of the only lakes in Oklahoma I have not seen is Tenkiller, and

222

I have heard it is really pretty. I got on my Honda Goldwing and rode to the little town of Vian, ten miles west of Sallisaw, then turned north on Highway 82. About four miles from town, at the top of a long hill, there was a little sign on the west side of the highway saying "property for sale by owner." It had a phone number, and I called. The fellow who answered said he would meet us there on Monday morning at 9:00 AM.

Casey Sullivan is the son of Dr. Sullivan of Vian and their family owned most of the property along Highway 82 for a couple of miles. We looked at a few lots along Farm Road 1010, then looked at some down the highway. When Diana and I saw the lots we liked, we told Casey to ask his father what would be the least amount they would take for the four lots we liked. We agreed on a price the next day, and we gave Casey earnest money and got the sale papers in order.

We headed back to Vegas to start planning how we were going to build the place and a new life in the Green Country, as it is called in Eastern Oklahoma. Green Country is curvy roads, nice trees, lakes and real grass. You see, Las Vegas is too hot for grass, so our yard had little rocks. No lawnmower or weed eater, just rocks. Oklahoma has grass and little critters that live in the woods and the lawns.

Diana calls them chicks and tigers. Ticks and chiggers live in all grassy areas of eastern Oklahoma, so I bought a spreader to put some stuff on the place to kill these chicks and tigers. No one likes ticks; most people know they carry things like Lyme disease and no one wants that. Now the chiggers are a different story; they are sometimes called no-see-ums because they are tiny little critters that crawl up your legs and nibble on your boys that reside in the fruit of the looms. Red bumps and a lot of scratching in places where you are not supposed to scratch in public.

We will overcome all the little things about the area and enjoy the heck out of living in a place with lakes, fishing, golf, rainy days, and all. We only needed to figure out what kind of place to build on the property we bought.

Now, I'm not a house person. I want a nice place to live but to build a large house with way too much floor space and too many bedrooms is a waste of money. We explored building a barndominium and decided it would cost far too much. Time was also a big factor because we didn't want to spend a year building a place to live. The redneck solution would be a double-wide trailer house with 1800 square feet, three bedrooms, and two baths. Yes, sir, that would fit the bill, and the casa would be ready to move into in about a week.

We bought the thing and headed back to Las Vegas to get everything ready to get this show on the road. We talked to a contractor who builds pole barns about a forty-by-forty shop. While in the town of Gore talking to the fellow who does the pole barns, I found a New Holland Diesel Tractor, mower and box blade so cheap I had to buy it.

Back in Las Vegas, the work was about to get serious with the upcoming move. Diana's father was moved to an assisted living place, so we needed to get rid of all the leftover items in his house so it could be rented. This turned out to be three weeks of real work. We held two open house sales that I would not care to ever do again. Then, we had two-yard sales at our house to get rid of all the items we didn't want to take with us to Oklahoma.

At the end of September, we headed back to Vian, Oklahoma, to get the land we purchased ready to move into. This was a cow pasture with trees, big trees on it, and nothing else. We had one month to make it into something we would want to live in. We started with the house, getting the foundation poured, and the house moved onto the property and set. This took about ten days of hell. I wanted the foundation done a little differently than was conventional, and this turned out to be a fight from start to finish. I won the fight with one statement to the guys that set the house, "Who is paying for this, you or me?" A concept they were not acquainted with yet. They would tell the customer this is how it is done, and most people would agree.

Then came all the utilities…electricity, water, and so on. The electric company tried to tell Diana that it would take two to three weeks to get a work order done on new service. Diana told them that the day after tomorrow was good for me, and they were there in two days and put in the electric pole and transformer, ready to hook up to the house. The same thing happened with the water company. We had water and electricity in three days, not three weeks.

I hired a fellow to work for me, building fences and gates and doing all that was needed to get the place ready. Simon is Mexican from Juarez, Mexico, but has lived in the US for many years. Simon is married and has four boys.

He is a very good worker, and without his help, we would not have done all the work necessary to build this place in one month.

We got everything ready to move in during the month of October 2012, then went back to Vegas to get everything ready to move to Oklahoma in December.

We did three garage sales in the month of November to get rid of unwanted stuff. Boy, did we have the stuff, a collection of twenty years in Vegas. We sold most of the living room furniture and all of the furniture in Diana's dad's home and then started loading what was left in our camper.

Next was loading the ABF trailer that was parked in front of our house. With trailers loaded, we left Vegas with a smile and started off on a new page in our lives in Eastern Oklahoma.

We arrived in Vian, Oklahoma, and the ABF trailer showed up a day later. How do I unload a big trailer with all this stuff? I went to the high school and got the wrestling team. These big boys had the trailer unloaded in less than two hours. The coach told me these guys could really use the money right before Christmas.

The first winter in Eastern Oklahoma was a lot different than in Las Vegas. Much colder, and a foot of snow. It's been a long time since we saw that much of the white stuff.

In March, I thought I should find a good Doctor. In talking with the locals, I was told by some of the people that Dr. Anderson in Gore was very good. I thought I should get a physical since I had not had one since all the stuff with my back four years earlier. This visit to the Doctor was going to be a lot more than I expected.

Dr. Anderson sent me to see a Doctor in Muskogee to get a colonoscopy. I wasn't too thrilled about the idea, but I made the appointment anyway. Well, this doctor looked at my colon, and to my surprise, he told me I have colon cancer. Now, cancer is not a word I wanted to hear. I have very little knowledge about medical things. I know only two medicines, Advil and Crown Royal. Hearing this news from the doctor would have normally scared me to death, but there was this little voice in my head that said, "Don't worry, I'll take care of it."

Well, I had colon cancer and had surgery the next month to fix it. Dr. Johnson in Tulsa fixed the problem, taking out ten inches of my colon and trying to fix a hernia all in the same surgery. The cancer was removed and had not spread, so it was a 100 percent fix. The doctor told me to do the hernia; he would just sew the heck out of things, and maybe it would work. He said he could not use mesh because he didn't want to mess with the colon. Too much risk of infection, he told me.

In June, I went back to the family doctor for a follow-up. He noticed a spot on my left leg below the knee. He said I should see a dermatologist. The doctor made an appointment with Johnson Dermatology in Ft. Smith, Arkansas.

It turned out to be melanoma skin cancer, and I would need surgery to fix this. Tulsa again and another doctor to whittle on me. He did, and it, too, had not spread, so it was a 100 percent fix also. Dr. Johnson in Fort Smith also removed two lesser skin cancers, one on my forehead and one on my neck. I was being cut on everywhere I went that year. Then, in January 2014, another doctor in Tulsa redid the hernia that did not get fixed. Let's see that is seven surgeries in less than one year.

I was getting ready for the seventies, cut up but going to be just fine. Ready for the golden years, I told myself nothing to worry about but all the things the seventies have for me. Golf and fishing are much better than recovering from getting cut on.

In September 2014, we thought it was time to get rid of the hot rods, the Cobra, and the Corvette. We took both to the Mecum Classic Car auction in Dallas, Texas, and both sold for more than we had in them. No more hot rods for a while. A fellow came by one day the next week and offered me enough money that he left the house with my Honda Goldwing motorcycle.

I went to Fort Smith the next week and bought a new Ram 1500 Hemi truck. The following week, we headed to Milwaukee for a high school reunion. Diana graduated from Greenfield High School in 1968, and they wanted to have a reunion for the first time since '68. We left our gold Dodge truck in Fort Smith to get new seat covers. On our way back home, we stopped to get the truck, and the owner had a hot rod Jeep for sale, cheap. This Jeep had over 60,000 dollars spent on hopping it up. It had a Dodge Hemi engine with over 400 horsepower and many other upgrades done to it. I gave $20,000 for it and an army trailer. Good deal if I had any use for the thing, which I did not. In one and a half years, it did not get over 150 miles put on it by us. I sold it for 28,750 dollars and am glad it is gone.

Well, sooner or later, the Big Bank was going to do something about the house in Las Vegas, even though they might not have the right to do anything. Sure enough, in October 2014, they broke into the house the week our last renter moved out. We got a police report on the break-in and decided to sue the Big Bank for damages, not only for the break-in but also for all the crap they have given us over the last four and a half years.

So, on January 7, 2015 we filed suit on the Big Bank for twelve and one-half million dollars.

Well, to make a long story short, we settled the lawsuit after the federal judge said to us in a meeting, "Who gives a damn that this bank harassed you." That told us we couldn't win the case, so we settled out of court.

#

Well to put an end to a long story, my life so far has had its ups and downs, but I never stayed down long enough for it to bother me. I have always been willing to move on to the next adventure; to learn a lot of different things and to simply try to enjoy. People always tell me that I am a very interesting guy. I enjoy sharing my experiences with everyone who will listen. Perhaps I'm not that unusual in all the things I have done. And I'm not done yet…life is an adventure which everyone should grab a piece of and enjoy!

And now, Trump has won the election and we shall all live happily ever after.

⧼About the Author⧽

Tom West lives in east central Oklahoma. He retired from the casino business in 2007. After 20 years of living in the fast lane in Las Vegas, Nevada, he calls the country his home and thoroughly enjoys it.

Tom started writing about his life experiences, although not diligently, shortly after retiring. It started as his history to pass on to his family. From his early days in Southwestern Oklahoma, where he was born during World War II, to his retirement years, he has written about the many things he has done and seen and the numerous people he has met along the way. Those who heard him talk about his life over the years have told him you are a very interesting person, and you should write a book. One such person was Dr. A.W. Sibley, an author himself. He is the one who suggested the title of for Tom's book "The most interesting man you have never met."

Tom also has co-authored a book for the US Government published by the Washington National Press. He wrote a speech for a US Senator given to a joint session of Congress for which Tom received a Congressional Commendation signed by the then President.

Married for 44 years, Tom and his wife have a very active lifestyle with a bass boat, motorcycle, and roadster sports car. And, of course, lots of traveling.

At 75 years old, Tom finished telling his story for all to enjoy. Now at 80, he states, "My life has been and is still interesting and exciting every day."